CELTIC QUILTING

GAIL LAWTHER

David & Charles

A DAVID & CHARLES BOOK

First published in the UK in 1998
First published in paperback 2002, reprinted 2003
Text and designs Copyright © Gail Lawther 1998, 2002
Photography and layout Copyright © David & Charles 1998, 2002

Distributed in North America by
F&W Publications, Inc., 4700 East Galbraith Road, Cincinnati, OH 45236
1-800-289-0963

A catalogue record for this book is available from the British Library.

ISBN 0 7153 1260 X

Photography by Di Lewis
Jacket photograph by Shona Wood
Book design by Christopher Lawther
Printed in Singapore by KHL Printing Co Pte Ltd
for David & Charles
Brunel House   Newton Abbot   Devon

137,105
£15.08

CONTENTS

Introduction   6

WHOLECLOTH   **14**
Greetings cards   16
Wholecloth silk cushion   19
Spiral-design dolls' quilt   22
Knotwork pram quilt   24
Birds sofa throw   29

APPLIQUE   **32**
Wedding ring cushion   34
Sparkling evening bag   37
Dragon picture   40
Shadow-work cot quilt   44
Stained glass wall hanging   48

TRAPUNTO   **54**
Triangular pincushion   56
Initial pictures   58
Herb pillow   62
Bridal handbag   65
Knotwork trinket box   68

PATCHWORK   **72**
Bright cushion   74
Geometric table-mats   76
Key-pattern footstool   79
Patchwork work-bag   82
Child's bed quilt   86

SASHIKO   **90**
Sashiko greetings cards   92
Red and gold needlecase   94
Indigo teacosy   97
Geometric tablecloth   99
Sashiko bed quilt   103

PATTERN LIBRARY   **108**
Knots   108
Knotwork borders   112
Spiral designs   116
Fret and key patterns   118
Alphabets   120
Carpet page designs   122
Animals, birds and fish   124
Plant designs   126

Acknowledgements   127
Bibliography   127
Index   128

ℐNTRODUCTION

Celtic designs have become increasingly popular over the past few years and stitchers – always on the look-out for new ideas and inspiration – haven't been slow in adapting some of the rich heritage of Celtic art to their own art form. Quilts and embroideries with Celtic inspirations have been on show at many of the national exhibitions, which has helped to spread appreciation of this period of history among stitchers. In 1996 David & Charles produced *Celtic Cross Stitch*, to a very enthusiastic reception, and I kept being asked when there was going to be an equivalent book for the patchwork and quilting market. *Celtic Quilting* is my answer!

For some reason the work of the Celtic artists fascinates us. Perhaps it's the combination of exquisitely decorative and expressive art, set in a time we know very little about, at the end of the Dark Ages. We think of the people living then as so primitive in many ways – this was even before the great flowering of art and technology in medieval times – and yet their illuminations, carvings and metalwork still have the power to take our breath away with their beauty. Born in the pagan religions of the Anglo-Saxon tribes, Celtic art found its full flowering with the sweep of Christianity across Western Europe, beginning in Ireland in the fifth and sixth centuries and continuing to the ninth and tenth centuries, blending almost imperceptibly into the early medieval period.

The Celtic art that has survived the centuries is mostly found on items of particular spiritual or religious significance, partly because these were made in more durable materials than everyday items, and partly because they were cherished because of their religious associations. As a result, we can still see today some of the artefacts that were probably considered, even at the time, as the pinnacles of Celtic art.

Knots and fretwork designs were probably carved crudely into everyday items, such as wooden serving bowls or simple bed-heads for reasonably well-off families, but these will have been chopped up for firewood as soon as they became too cracked or soiled to be useful. The items that have survived down the ages include things like the spectacular hoard of jewellery buried at Sutton Hoo, the carvings on reliquaries and caskets kept in monasteries and abbeys, and the exquisite illuminations of manuscripts such as the *Book of Kells*, the Lindisfarne Gospels and the *Book of Durrow*.

METHODS OF QUILTING

There are many different quilting methods and subsidiary techniques within those. For this book I have chosen five main types of quilting and designed a series of projects suitable for each. Each section begins with an introduction, which looks at the basic skills unique to that technique and the kind of designs that work best for it. There are a few general techniques common to most types of quilting; these are described in Before You Begin, and are cross-referred within the projects. There is also a handy section on page 13, which describes the stitches used in the various projects.

The first section deals with **wholecloth quilting**, sometimes called English quilting, which involves stitching a pattern onto a single piece of backing cloth that has been padded with wadding.

The second section covers **appliqué**, which at its most basic is the principle of laying a shaped piece of fabric onto a backing and attaching it with stitching. Several different methods of appliqué are used for the projects, including shadow appliqué, stained glass appliqué and machine appliqué.

The third section is **trapunto**, or stuffed quilting. Most of the projects within this section use the corded technique, where channels are stitched onto a double layer of fabric and then padded by threading them with yarn or cord.

The fourth section covers **patchwork**, or piecing, which involves stitching together patches of fabrics in varying colours or designs so that they form a decorative pattern. The projects here use several different patchwork techniques, including strip-piecing and piecing over papers.

The fifth section is **sashiko**, a Japanese method of decorative stitching in which patterns are produced on lightly padded background fabric by working lines of running stitch in a contrasting colour. The section contains Celtic designs adapted for sashiko stitching.

At the end of the book, on pages 108–126, there is a **pattern library** of extra Celtic designs that don't appear in the worked projects. You can use these to create your own Celtic quilting projects, either using them as they are, mixing them or adapting them to suit your own preferences. At the end of the book you'll find a bibliography of useful books relating to Celtic art. These are all excellent for inspiration and some show how to construct both simple and more complicated examples.

The examples on the right show how different the same simple Celtic design can look when the basic lines are adapted and the whole design is worked in different quilting methods. This shows how easily you can vary many of the projects in the book by transferring a design from one technique to another, and some of the ways in which you can adapt the designs shown in the pattern library.

A   *The basic knot design, a simple pattern made up of three separate strands.*

B   *How the knot would look stitched in wholecloth quilting, with tiny quilting stitches following the different lines of the pattern.*

C   *Appliqué in several different fabrics could give this appearance.*

D   *Here the knot has been turned into a double line which could be worked as corded quilting.*

E   *Simple piecing turns the knot into a patchwork project.*

F   *Bold sashiko stitching in a contrasting colour brings out the lines of the knot.*

G   *In this version a double border has been added. This could be used for stained glass appliqué, or for wholecloth, sashiko or corded quilting.*

H   *The corners of the knot have been altered here, making it look quite different.*

I   *In this example two of the basic knots have been positioned side by side, and their strands interwoven, to produce a larger, rectangular knot that could be stitched on its own or worked into a border.*

CELTIC DESIGN INSPIRATION

The intricate knots are probably the designs that most people think of when they consider Celtic art, but if you browse through a facsimile of one of the illuminated manuscripts, it soon becomes obvious that the artists of the time used many different kinds of design and decoration. Let's look at some of these styles and consider how they can be adapted for different quilting techniques.

KNOTWORK

The flowing lines of Celtic knots, simple or complex, are a quilter's dream. Once the design is transferred to the fabric, the lines can be quilted following the interweaving of the knots, making them very  easy to stitch in wholecloth quilting or in sashiko. Large, complex knots interpreted in wholecloth quilting can be thrown into relief by working background textures behind them, or be emphasised by double lines of stitching round the outside. The wholecloth silk cushion on page 19 uses this technique to make the knot stand out. The stitching can be in the same colour as the background, as it is for the knotwork pram quilt on page 24, or worked in one or more colours, as it is in the greetings cards on page 16 and the birds sofa throw on page 29.

Knotwork designs are also wonderful for trapunto, or stuffed, quilting, especially the corded technique. Once again it's very easy to follow the line or lines of the design with the padding if each part of the knot pattern is outlined on both sides to create a channel.

Several different appliqué methods can be used to produce knotwork designs on quilts. The method used for the wedding ring cushion on page 34, which produces the appearance of an interweaving knot with just one piece of fabric, can be adapted to work with any knotwork pattern. The technique used for the shadow-work cot quilt on page 44 is not dissimilar: here the knot shapes are cut from

fabric and laid under a sheer top fabric, and hand quilting over the top gives the impression of the interweaving lines. It is also possible to use the stained glass technique, as for the birds wall hanging on page 48, to outline large knot designs, laying down a piece of bias binding on each side of the line followed by the knot.

Knotwork is quite difficult to produce in patchwork, because the lines of many knot patterns are curved. However, with patience and a little ingenuity, knots can be pieced from regular patches such as squares, rectangles and triangles, as shown in the work-bag on page 82.

One of the main challenges in producing good knotwork quilts is in drawing the original design. The lines of the knot should be smoothly drawn and consistent, whether they are straight or curved. Knots designs are constructed in many different ways – for instance mirror images, four identical quarters, 180° rotations, identical segments in a circle – and if you are adapting a knot from another source, you will need to look at it carefully to see how it is formed. Working on a grid will help as you draw up the basic design and the same goes for knots that you construct yourself from scratch. There are short-cuts, too. For example, if your knot is constructed from four identical quarters, draw one quarter correctly and then take several photocopies and splice them together. I've also discovered that computer graphics programs are extremely useful!

There are several ways of decorating basic knotwork designs if you want to make them more complex. The lines of the knot may be single, as in the wholecloth silk cushion on page 19, or multiple, as in the double line used for the triangular pincushion on page 56. To create a multiple knot, simply divide the main line of the knot evenly into the required number of channels. You can work the interweaving of these lines so that they all follow the same pattern, or so that they weave over and under independently.

If you make the line of the knot itself quite wide, you will have room inside it to stitch a subsidiary pattern, such as in the sashiko knot card on page 92. Alternatively, you can throw the knot into relief with stitching outside it, as I've done with the herb pillow on page 62. This design also makes use of decorative finials where some of the lines finish. In many knotwork designs the lines are continuous, but on patterns where the ends of lines are shown, the Celtic artists usually swelled them into floral tips. The initial pictures on page 58–61 also use decorative finials.

SPIRALS

Spiral designs are much more easily adapted to quilting than to a counted thread form of stitchery such as cross stitch. The essential character of spiral designs comes from their strong, exuberant curves spinning out from one or more centres. These strong lines make them very satisfactory to stitch, and once again the lines are easy to reproduce in wholecloth quilting and in sashiko, particularly. The red and gold needlecase on page 94 and the spiral-design dolls' quilt on page 22 are both created from this type of spiral pattern.

Although the spiral patterns look at first sight as though they'd be ideal for corded trapunto work, they don't always work too well in their original form. This is because, unlike knot designs, the spiral patterns often introduce extra lines which join the main lines of the pattern, or single lines that are not paired with matching lines to create channels. With a bit of creativity, though, some spiral designs can be adapted to work with this technique. The bridal handbag on page 65 uses a knotwork border that is based on a loose spiral pattern. The same kind of loose spiral is used for the knotwork circle on the wedding ring cushion on page 34. Some of the more intricate spiral patterns could be interpreted in appliqué patches in several different colours, stitched by hand or machine. Spiral designs don't lend themselves very easily to patchwork, unless you are adept at stitching complex curved seams!

If you want to design your own radiating Celtic patterns, have a look through some of the source books suggested in the bibliography on page 127 and make some sketches. The construction of some of the designs is very complex, especially when there are several spirals that flow into each other,

and they can be quite difficult to create – or even to copy! Some form circular designs, some flow into rectangles or squares, and others create borders which can be extended *ad infinitum*. If you are creating designs for wholecloth or sashiko quilting, keep the lines simple: a few, clearly defined lines that join each other at specific points will look much more effective than a swarm of indistinct pattern lines.

CARPET PAGE PATTERNS

This rather strange term describes the very large, intricate designs that were created by Celtic illuminators to fill whole pages – rather as we might have a full-page photograph as a frontispiece to a book. The appearance of the pages made them look like colourful and elaborate stitched carpets, hence the name. These pages often contained many forms of decoration together – perhaps knots, animals, fret and key patterns all in the same piece of artwork – but they were always arranged on a mathematical grid. Sometimes the grid is invisible and can only be seen when the pattern is analysed: sometimes it is part of the pattern, in the form of squares, rectangles, circles and stepped designs. This kind of pattern is the inspiration behind the sparkling evening bag on page 37, the bright cushion on page 74, and the child's bed quilt on page 86.

Carpet patterns can be worked in just about any method of quilting – the lines could be worked in wholecloth quilting or sashiko very easily. However, the strong lines make them some of the best Celtic patterns for interpretation in appliqué, and also for patchwork, because they can be pieced very simply. The wonderful fabrics available today, such as the metallics used for the evening bag and the gold print designs used for the bright cushion, make it easy to capture some of the richness of the original patterns, and as some of the projects in the book show, the finished designs can be encrusted with beads, buttons and fake jewels.

If you are interested in designing your own carpet patterns, look through facsimiles of Celtic illuminated manuscripts and sketch the grids used for the carpet pages – the shapes are usually easy to construct with rulers and protractors. Alternatively, delve into some of the books mentioned on page 127 which talk about how the large patterns are constructed. If you are feeling brave, you could add knotwork or animal designs to your basic carpet-page layout.

FRET AND KEY PATTERNS

Although we tend to associate the key pattern with the Greeks, it existed in many ancient civilisations, including prehistoric Africa, ancient Egypt and ancient Rome. Perhaps it was the Romans  who introduced it to Britain, ready for it to re-emerge in Celtic art! Fret and key patterns appear in many different forms in Celtic art, both simple and complex repeats worked into borders and individual motifs. The indigo teacosy on page 97 shows an example of a border and a matching single motif. The designs vary enormously. They may be created from squares or rectangles, like the footstool on page 79, or from triangles and wedges like the geometric tablecloth design on page 99. Some of the most beautiful and complex key patterns are worked into a circle, with complex curved and angled lines. The sashiko card on page 92 is an example of this kind of design.

The strong lines of the key patterns make them very easy to interpret in all kinds of quilting. Once again, the lines can be double so that they produce actual channels, like the designs used for the tablecloth and the teacosy, or they can be worked as single lines like the circular card. If the line is double it can, of course, be padded with trapunto quilting. If you use this method, make sure that you take the padding right into the angles and corners formed by the design so that they are filled out well.

Fret patterns based on rectangles and squares work very well in American patchwork. The footstool on page 79 is pieced in this way, building up the rows of the central design from patches of fabric, then joining the rows into a block and surrounding it with borders. Designs like this can be worked at different scales – a simple fret or key design worked in large patches could be used to create a bed quilt in a day. If you are creating your own design of this kind, the main trick is to work out the piecing order carefully so that you can stitch everything with straight seams.

With all fret and key patterns, accuracy is important. They are all based on strict mathematical grids. In some, this grid is very obvious but in others, especially the circular designs, it may take some working out. The books which have sections on constructing Celtic art are very helpful for showing the basic construction lines that underlie some of the more unusual designs of this kind.

ANIMALS, BIRDS AND FISH

The Celts are famous for their extraordinary biomorphic designs – ones that imitate living things. Sometimes these imitations are scarcely recognisable, for instance the weird sea-horse and reptile  designs that appear on some manuscripts and carvings. Even when the basic animal is readily recognised, it is often twisted into its own elaborate knotwork or spiral without any regard for anatomy, so the legs or crests of birds and the feet or tongues of dogs create their own pattern as they twist and turn across the design. Birds in particular provide the opportunity for extra decoration in the form of their feathers, wings and crests. When fish occasionally appear in Celtic designs they are usually also highly decorated. Sometimes though, the designs are touchingly life-like and beautiful depictions can be found in Celtic art of horses (and horsemen), angels, deer, boar, bulls and dogs.

Because the biomorphic designs are so elaborate, their use in quilting is limited to techniques where strong, irregular lines can be created. Wholecloth quilting and sashiko are obvious examples, for instance the birds sofa throw on page 29 and the card on page 92. Stuffed or trapunto versions of these designs would also work well. Animal and bird depictions are good too for appliqué, as the dragon picture on page 40 and the birds wall hanging on page 48 show. Machine appliqué or stained glass patchwork can be adapted to virtually any design, as both techniques allow a lot of freedom in the way the lines are formed. The regular lines of patchwork are not really a suitable technique for reproducing the complicated Celtic biomorphic designs.

Animal and bird designs abound in Celtic art, so if you want to create your own you will find plenty of sources of inspiration. Many of these depictions are extremely complex though, and you may have to isolate one or two elements and simplify them. The biomorphic designs I have used for this book are simplified greatly from their original sources, because otherwise the lines would have been too difficult to work with. You can have great fun experimenting though, and creating your own reptiles, birds and sea-horses!

LETTERING

The letterforms in Celtic Bible manuscripts are among the most beautiful in the world. Everyone admires the fantastic illuminated initials as artworks in their own right, but only the most dedicated of stitchers would choose one of these letters to adapt for embroidery or quilting! However, the scribes of this time also produced excellent 'text' letterforms: simple in character, beautifully formed and very attractive to look at. I've taken just one of these uncial alphabets and adapted it for quilting in the initial pictures on page 58. These can be personalised with any of the letterforms from the alphabet on the succeeding pages. In this project the letters are stitched onto a double layer of fabric and then stuffed from behind with coloured yarn so that the colours show through the top, sheer layers.

The letterforms could be used with other kinds of quilting too. Inevitably the lines of letters work best with one of the linear types of stitching, such as wholecloth or sashiko. If you wanted to produce a single, elaborate initial you could copy one from a manuscript and simplify some of the lines to adapt it for quilting. You may also find that some of the simpler letters will adapt to corded quilting.

BEFORE YOU BEGIN. . .

MATERIALS AND EQUIPMENT

If you are completely new to quilting, you might wonder where you start and whether you need any special equipment. The answers are very reassuring. Quilting is very easy to master and the only equipment that is essential are things that you will already have in your sewing kit – sharp scissors, pins, a range of needles. There are many extra items that are available for quilters to make particular tasks easier, but very few of them are needed for the projects in this book.

Extra Equipment
There are a few pieces of equipment that you will probably find useful.
- A water-soluble marking pen, the marks from which disappear when sprayed with cold water.
- A fading pen, the marks from which disappear after a day.
- A rotary cutter and board, which make cutting accurate squares and strips much easier than doing it with scissors.
- A thimble, even if you don't normally use one, is useful when hand quilting, as all the repetitive stitching can take its toll on the fingertips!
- A lightbox is ideal for transferring designs onto dark fabrics. Alternatively, dressmakers' carbon paper is very useful – use a colour a few shades lighter or darker than your background fabric.

Fabrics
Each project will tell you what fabrics are necessary for that particular item and how to prepare them. Generally, if an item is going to need to be laundered, the fabrics should be washed before you use them. This will remove any dressing and soften the fabric and also make sure that it is colourfast. If a fabric continues to 'bleed' after several rinses, discard it and choose another one instead. If the item does not need to be washable (for instance a picture or an evening bag), the fabric will not need to be washed beforehand. Press fabrics before you cut or mark them as this makes it easier to cut or mark accurate shapes.

The fabrics that work best for quilting and patchwork are firmly woven ones such as cotton, cotton/polyester mixes, silk and polyester silk imitations. Fabrics such as satins and metallics require special care as they fray readily and can slither out of shape.

Threads

Special quilting thread is available in a wide range of colours; this is a firm, quite thick cotton thread that copes well with being pulled through the layers of fabric numerous times. It is also possible to quilt small items with ordinary cotton or cotton/polyester sewing thread. For techniques in which you want the stitches to show more, such as trapunto and sashiko, you could also try using stranded cottons, coton à broder and the different thicknesses of coton perlé. Special sashiko thread is also available, but it only comes in white. Metallic thread is effective in quilting but needs to be used with care as it shreds easily.

GENERAL TECHNIQUES

There are a few techniques which are used in most types of quilting and in general relate to the preparation of a project. These are given page references within the projects, referring you back here if need be.

Enlarging Designs

For the project designs that are too large to be included in the book at actual size, you will need a satisfactory method of enlarging the design. Photocopiers are extremely useful for this. Where relevant, each design includes a percentage figure which tells you how much to enlarge it by if you are using a photocopier. For designs that need to be very large (for instance the sofa throw on page 29 and the sashiko bed quilt on page 103), and for enlarging without the aid of a photocopier, each design also gives the finished dimension of the design at actual size.

You can also successfully enlarge a design by the grid method. For example, to quadruple the area of a design, draw a grid of 1cm squares in pencil over the design. On a piece of paper draw another grid of 2cm squares and copy the design by hand onto the new grid to produce a new pattern that is four times the area of the original.

Centring Designs on Fabric

To ensure that a design is transferred to the exact centre of a piece of fabric, fold the fabric in half lengthways and then widthways and mark the two fold lines with lines of tacking or fading pen marks. Use these as guides for positioning the design.

Marking Designs on Fabric

There are various ways to transfer a design to fabric. If the fabric is relatively pale, you will often be able to lay it over a design and trace the lines. If the fabric is darker, a lightbox will allow you to see the lines through it. Dressmakers' carbon paper is also useful. Choose a shade or colour slightly darker or lighter than your fabric, lay it carbon side down on the front of the fabric and lay the design on top, then trace over the design lines with a pencil.

Using a Quilting Frame

Whether you are quilting by hand or machine, the fabric needs to be stretched so that the wadding is spread evenly all the time and the stitching is kept at a constant tension. If you don't keep the fabric taut as you stitch, the design will often pull unevenly around the stitching. The best way of keeping it taut is in a quilting frame. Hand-held frames are like large embroidery hoops and the fabric is spread over them in the same way. Rolling frames are used for large quilts and are large floor-standing frames which allow one part of the quilt to be stitched while the rest is rolled up out of the way at the sides. With both hand and machine quilting, the best method is to begin at the centre of the design and work outwards; this makes it easier to keep the wadding distributed evenly as you stitch.

Making Up

Each section of the book describes and illustrates any necessary techniques that are specific to that quilting method. Any other techniques you need – for instance, how to make up a simple cushion cover – are covered in the relevant project.

If you have never quilted before, begin with one of the easy project such as the cards on page 16 or 92, the dolls' quilt on page 22, the pincushion on page 56, the needlecase on page 94, or the patchwork cushion on page 74. If you are an experienced quilter, you will be able to tackle any of the projects straight away.

I had great fun designing and making the projects in this book, and researching all the patterns for them. I hope you really enjoy them too!

A *Chain stitch creates a thick outline with loops of stitching, and can be useful for making the stitched channels in threaded trapunto quilting.*

B *Whipped running stitch creates a stronger outline than running stitch on its own; the thread used for the whipping can be the same as the one used for the running stitch, or can be a contrasting colour or texture. The final stitch looks like a fine twisted cord.*

C *Backstitch forms a solid stitching line when you want a more definite outline for certain parts of a design.*

D *Seeding is a way of creating texture, and involves making tiny straight stitches at random angles on the background fabric. Seeding is a good way of throwing quilted designs into relief on small items.*

E *Ladder stitch is useful for invisibly closing gaps in seams, for example when you have turned out a pincushion or herb pillow. It is made by taking a straight stitch along each seam allowance alternately.*

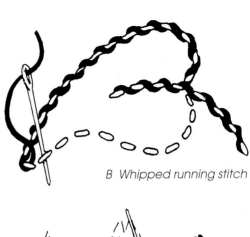

B Whipped running stitch

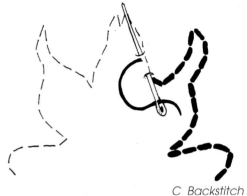

C Backstitch

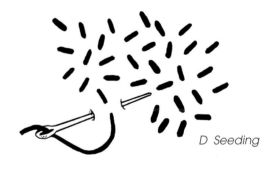

D Seeding

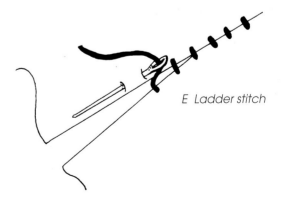

E Ladder stitch

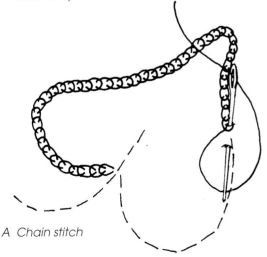

A Chain stitch

W'HOLECLOTH

Wholecloth quilting (sometimes known as English quilting) is one of the oldest quilting methods and, as the name implies, a single piece of background fabric is used. Sometimes, when a l... is required, several sections may be seamed to produce... piece, but the piecing is practical rather than decorat... unlike patchwork it is not supposed to be notice...

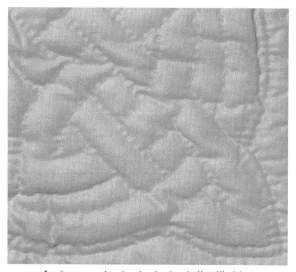

A close-up look at wholecloth stitching

The background fabric is usually plain, though occasionally a very small print is used. The idea is to have as simple a background as possible because the decoration comes from the elaborate patterns produced by the quilting stitches. In the north of England, which in past centuries produced many of the most superb wholecloth quilts, the bedcovers kept for 'best' were white-on-white – white quilting on a plain white or pale cream cotton background. Any colour can be used though, and in this chapter as well as cream fabrics I have used a pale buttercup yellow for the pram quilt on page 24, a gently marbled blue and peach fabric for the dolls' quilt on page 22, and a stunning dark plum silk for the cushion on page 19.

WHOLECLOTH DESIGNS

Traditional wholecloth design... items such as leaves, flowers, ... fans. Some ancient patterns al... plaited or knotwork borders, ar... designs known as True Lovers... Celtic-style knots. Not surpri... Celtic designs also look very... wholecloth quilting; the flowin... shapes and spirals are easy... straight or slightly curved lines... work well.

All the designs from this who... be adapted to other technique... the spiral design of the dolls... good worked in sashiko, and... from the silk cushion coul... smaller scale as a threaded kn...

WHOLECLOTH QUILTING TE...

The basic technique for wh... very simple. The design is... background in the most ap... page 12), and a 'sandwich' is... (marked) layer of fabric, a laye... background fabric. The backgr... the one that will actually back the finished project, or it may be an extra lining layer of muslin. This 'sandwich' is then tacked together with horizontal and vertical rows of tacking in a grid pattern (see Fig A), which holds the three layers together while they are being quilted and stops the wadding from moving and bunching up. For large quilts the rows of tacking can be about 2–3in (5–7.5cm) apart; for smaller projects, they should be rather closer together.

Tacking guns are now available which shoot small plastic tags through the quilt layers (see Fig B); these are then cut and removed after the stitching is completed. If you want to use a tacking gun, try it out on a sample of your fabrics first to check that it does not make holes that are too noticeable.

Before you start the actual quilting, whether by hand or machine, the fabric needs to be taut so that the wadding is spread evenly and the stitching is kept at a constant tension. The use of a quilting frame achieves this and there are several types available.

HAND QUILTING

The stitching on wholecloth quilts can be done by hand or machine. Hand quilting is very attractive and soothing to do, though of course more time-consuming. If you are quilting by hand, the basic quilting stitch is an even running stitch which passes through all layers of your 'sandwich' (see Fig C). Begin each thread with a knot at the back which you pull through the backing fabric into the wadding (see Fig D), and end each thread with a knot on the front which you then pull down through the top fabric into the wadding (see Fig E).

The most versatile thread for hand quilting is proper quilting thread, but other threads can be used for different effects (see page 12).

MACHINE QUILTING

Wholecloth quilting can also be done by machine. In this case use an ordinary sewing thread or, if you prefer, a metallic thread. For long lines of stitching set your machine to a medium-length straight stitch; for complicated designs, drop the feed dog, attach an embroidery foot, and manipulate the fabric by hand to follow the marked pattern, keeping the curves of the design as smooth as possible.

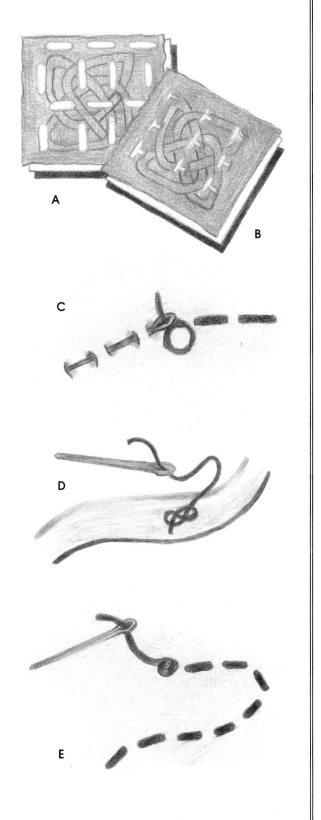

A

B

C

D

E

GREETINGS CARDS

Home-made cards are always popular and these three attractive designs are unusual enough for a special occasion, yet surprisingly quick and easy to stitch. All the designs use basic wholecloth quilting – running stitch on a lightly padded background to provide some extra texture for the pattern.

SIZE OF FINISHED DESIGNS: cross design 3in (7.5cm) diameter; key pattern 2¼in (6cm) square; hunting dog 3 x 2in (7.5 x 5cm)

MATERIALS

FOR THE CROSS DESIGN:
- ❖ *Green card blank with circular aperture 3¼in (8.25cm) in diameter*
- ❖ *Cream cotton fabric, 5in (13cm) square*
- ❖ *Green quilting or sewing thread*
- ❖ *Fine gold thread, eg Madeira No. 40 gold 6*
- ❖ *Water-soluble pen*

FOR THE KEY PATTERN:
- ❖ *Cream card blank with square aperture 2½in (6.5cm)*
- ❖ *Red silk fabric, 5in (13cm) square*
- ❖ *Cream quilting or sewing thread*
- ❖ *Fine gold thread, eg Madeira No. 40 gold 6*
- ❖ *10 small gold beads*
- ❖ *Pink crayon, slightly lighter than the fabric, or dressmakers' carbon paper*

FOR THE HUNTING DOG DESIGN:
- ❖ *Cream card blank with rectangular aperture 3 x 2in (7.5 x 5cm)*
- ❖ *Light green cotton fabric, 5 x 4in (13 x 10cm)*
- ❖ *Dark brown, light brown and medium green sewing or quilting threads*
- ❖ *Green crayon, slightly darker than your fabric*
- ❖ *Black felt-tip pen*

FOR ALL THE DESIGNS:
- ❖ *Sewing/tacking needle and thread*
- ❖ *Thin wadding*
- ❖ *Craft glue*

PRODUCING THE DESIGNS

THE CROSS DESIGN:

1 Trace the cross design below onto paper. Press the cream fabric. Lay the tracing on a flat surface, position the fabric over the top and trace the lines with the water-soluble pen.

2 Cut a piece of wadding to the same size as the fabric, put it behind the design and tack the layers together around the marked design.

3 Using the green quilting or sewing thread, stitch around all the lines of the design with small running stitches through the two layers.

4 Use the gold thread to stitch another line of quilting ⅛in (2mm) outside the edges of the cross shape, following the slight curves at the tip of each arm of the cross. When the stitching is complete, spray the design lightly with cold water to remove the water-soluble pen marks, and allow to dry completely.

THE KEY PATTERN DESIGN:

1 Trace the key pattern on page 17 onto paper. Press the red silk square and use a lightbox and the pink crayon (or dressmakers' carbon paper) to transfer the design to the fabric.

2 Cut a piece of wadding to the same size as the fabric, put it behind the design and tack the layers together around the marked design.

3 Using the cream quilting or sewing thread, stitch around all the lines of the design with small running stitches, keeping the lines as straight as possible while you stitch.

4 Attach the gold beads in the positions marked on the design, using two strands of the gold thread to secure them.

THE HUNTING DOG DESIGN:

1 Trace the dog design below right onto paper and then go over the lines with black felt-tip pen to make them darker. Press the fabric and lay it over the design, then trace the lines of the design with green crayon.

2 Cut a piece of wadding to the same size as the fabric, put it behind the design and tack the layers together around the marked design.

3 Using the dark brown thread, stitch around the lines of the dog with small running stitches. Stitch the tree shape with green thread, and the lines of the hills with mid brown thread.

TO COMPLETE ALL THREE CARDS:

Centre the cross design in the aperture of the green card and trim the fabric so that it is roughly 3/8in (1cm) larger all round than the aperture. Spread a little craft glue round only the edge of the aperture on the reverse side and stick the design in place. Fold over the inner flap of the card and secure round the edges with glue. Assemble the key pattern design and the hunting dog design in their appropriate card blanks in the same way.

WHOLECLOTH SILK CUSHION

Silk is wonderful to quilt – the needle passes quickly and easily through the fabric, turning even a complex knot like this one into a speedy design. For extra emphasis, this design is quilted in coton à broder thread in a slightly lighter shade than the dark plum of the silk, and the whole knot is thrown into relief by an extra line of quilting just outside the design. If you prefer, you could use contrasting colours for the background fabric and for the quilting.

SIZE OF FINISHED CUSHION: 21in (54cm) square
KNOT DESIGN SIZE: 13in (33cm) diameter

MATERIALS

❖ Plum-coloured silk, 1yd (1m) by at least 45in (115cm) wide
❖ One skein of coton à broder thread, slightly lighter than your fabric
❖ Muslin, 22in (56cm) square
❖ 2oz wadding, 22in (56cm) square
❖ Medium sewing needle
❖ Plum-coloured sewing thread
❖ Cushion pad, 18in (46cm) square
❖ Pink crayon, slightly lighter than your silk fabric
❖ Pencil, paper and black felt-tip pen for drawing the design
❖ Dressmakers' carbon paper (optional)
❖ Quilting hoop or frame (optional)

PRODUCING THE DESIGN

1 Enlarge the knot design on pages 20–21 to the correct size (see page 12), and go over the lines in black felt-tip pen to make them darker.

2 From the silk cut one 22in (56cm) square and two rectangles measuring 15 x 22in (38 x 56cm). Fold the silk square in half and then into quarters and press the crossing of the folds lightly to mark the exact centre, then unfold. Use dressmakers' carbon paper, or a lightbox and crayon, to transfer the design to the right side of the square of silk, making sure that the design is centred exactly (see page 12).

3 Lay the muslin on a flat surface and lay the wadding on top. Position the marked silk square, right side up, on top of the wadding and smooth the layers so that they are all totally flat. Pin the three layers together, then tack them with an even grid of horizontal and vertical lines of tacking stitches about 2–3in (5–7.5cm) apart (see page 14). Remove the pins from the work.

4 Using the coton à broder, and working with a quilting hoop or frame if you wish, begin quilting around the lines of the design using small, even quilting stitches (see page 15). Begin in the centre of the knot and work outwards. When the knot is complete, stitch another line of quilting 1/4in (5mm) outside the edges of the shape. Remove the tacking threads.

5 Press under and stitch a small double hem on one long side of each of the silk rectangles. Lay the quilted design, right side up, on a flat surface and place the two rectangles, right sides down, on top so that the hemmed edges overlap and the two shapes align with the edges of the square. Pin, tack and stitch a 1/2in (1cm) hem all round the edges. Clip the corners and trim the seam allowances to just beyond the stitching line, then turn the cushion cover right side out and press the very edges only so that you do not flatten the wadding.

6 Tack a line 1 1/2in (4cm) in from each edge, then topstitch round this line to produce an Oxford-style cushion cover with a flat border (see photograph). Insert the cushion pad, which will fill out the centre of the cushion.

PRACTICAL TIP

✧ *It's quite useful to wash the silk before you use it, as you will want to wash the cushion cover occasionally. Silk is often not colourfast, so wash it gently by hand in tepid soapy water and rinse it thoroughly until the water runs clear. When the complete cushion cover is washed, ideally this should be done by hand using a mild washing liquid suitable for silk.*

13in (33cm)
If you are using a
photocopier enlarge
by 140%

✧ **VARIATIONS** ✧

This knot is very adaptable and would work well
in the centre of square blocks for a large
patchwork quilt. You could also work it in pastel
silk appliqué as an alternative design for the
wedding ring cushion on page 34.

*In this detail you can see the extra line of quilting
stitches added outside the main knot; this throws
the central design into greater relief*

137, 105

SPIRAL-DESIGN DOLLS' QUILT

Simple spiral designs can look very striking worked in wholecloth quilting, as this dolls' quilt shows. The pattern is adapted from a spiral border: the central spiral flows out into four subsidiary ones and is set off by leaf shapes and circles. The background is a piece of plain white fabric that I marbled with blue and peach fabric paints, but any slightly mottled fabric will do. The back of this quilt features the spiral pattern on plain navy fabric.

SIZE OF FINISHED QUILT: 13¹/2 x 9in (34 x 23cm)

MATERIALS

❖ Blue and peach marbled or mottled cotton fabric, 13¹/2 x 9in (34 x 23cm)

❖ Navy blue cotton backing fabric, 15 x 10¹/2in (38 x 27cm)
❖ 2oz wadding, 13¹/2 x 9in (34 x 23cm)
❖ Navy blue quilting or sewing thread
❖ Medium sewing needle
❖ Black felt-tip pen
❖ Water-soluble pen
❖ Quilting hoop or frame (optional)

PRODUCING THE DESIGN

1 Wash and press the top and backing fabrics. Enlarge the spiral pattern opposite to the correct size (see page 12). Go over the lines with thick black felt-tip pen to make them darker. Lay the marbled or mottled fabric right side up over the

pattern so that there is an even border of fabric all round the design, and trace the lines using the water-soluble pen.

2 Lay the navy blue backing fabric right side down on a flat surface and lay the wadding on top so that there is an even border of fabric all round. Position the marked fabric, right side up, on top of the wadding, and smooth the layers so that they are all totally flat. Pin the three layers together, then tack them with an even grid of horizontal and vertical lines of tacking about 2in (5cm) apart (see page 14). Remove the pins from the work.

3 Using the navy blue quilting or sewing thread, and working with a hoop or frame if you wish (see page 12), begin quilting around the lines of the design using small, even quilting stitches (see page 15). Begin in the middle of the central large spiral and work outwards, keeping the lines of the curves smooth. Complete all of the spiral and leaf design before quilting the small circles.

When all the lines of the design are complete, remove the tacking threads.

4 Lay the design on a surface that will not cause running or staining – for instance a clean Formica worktop or a clean towel – and spray it all over with cold water to remove the marks left by the water-soluble pen. Leave to dry completely. If any pen marks remain, simply spray the design again and leave to dry.

5 Fold the navy blue fabric over the front of the design in a double hem so that the raw edges of the top fabric and wadding are enclosed. Tack in position. Slipstitch the edge of the hem to the quilt top with the navy thread.

PRACTICAL TIP

✧ *If you want to use a frame while quilting, you will find that an ordinary quilting frame is too big so use a large embroidery frame instead, but don't tighten the outside ring too much or it will mark the fabric.*

13in (33cm)

If you are using a photocopier enlarge by 205%

KNOTWORK PRAM QUILT

Traditional wholecloth quilting is given a Celtic twist in this exquisite pram quilt, with a trio of complex knots and a plaited border stitched by hand on a pale buttercup yellow background. Although the design looks ornate, it is very easy and quite quick to stitch, and the washable fabrics and wadding make it practical too. It's beautiful enough for an heirloom, but practical enough for everyday use.

SIZE OF FINISHED QUILT: 28$\frac{1}{2}$ x 19$\frac{1}{2}$in (72.5 x 49.5cm)

MATERIALS

- ❖ *1yd (1m) pale yellow glazed cotton fabric, at least 48in (122cm) wide*
- ❖ *2oz polyester wadding, 21 x 30in (53.5 x 76cm)*
- ❖ *White or cream muslin, the same size as the wadding*
- ❖ *Pale yellow quilting thread*
- ❖ *Yellow sewing thread*
- ❖ *Tacking thread*
- ❖ *Medium sewing needle*
- ❖ *Pencil, paper and black felt-tip pen for enlarging the pattern*
- ❖ *Water-soluble pen*
- ❖ *Quilting hoop or frame (optional)*

PRODUCING THE DESIGN

1 Wash and press the yellow fabric. From it cut one rectangle 21 x 30in (53.5 x 76cm), making sure that the long edges of the rectangle are parallel with the selvedges.

2 Enlarge the pattern on pages 26–27 to the correct size (see page 12). Go over the design with a black felt-tip pen so the lines are clear. Place the yellow cotton right side up over the design and pin in position so that there is an equal border of fabric all round the edges of the pattern. Trace the design lines onto the fabric using a water-soluble pen.

3 Lay the muslin on a flat surface and lay the wadding on top. Position the marked yellow cotton fabric, right side up, on top of the wadding and smooth the layers so that they are all totally flat. Pin the three layers together, then tack them with an even grid of horizontal and vertical lines of tacking about 2–3in (5–7.5cm) apart (see page 14). Remove the pins.

4 Using the yellow quilting thread, and working with a quilting hoop or frame if you wish (see page 12), begin quilting around the lines of the design using small, even quilting stitches (see page 15). Begin in the middle of the central large knot and work outwards. Complete all the three large knots before working on the border. When you come to the border, stitch the inside straight edge first, then the knotwork, then the outside straight edge. When all lines of the design are complete, remove the tacking threads carefully without pulling.

5 Lay the design on a surface that will not cause running or staining (eg, a clean Formica worktop or a clean towel) and spray it all over with cold water to remove the marks left by the water-soluble pen. Leave to dry completely. If any pen marks remain, simply spray the design again and leave to dry.

6 From the remaining yellow fabric, cut a rectangle 23 x 32in (58.5 x 81.5cm). Lay this right side down on a flat surface, and lay the quilted design, right side up, on top so that there is an even border of fabric all around the quilt top. Pin or tack the three layers together. Using the yellow quilting thread as before, quilt highlighting lines 1/4in (5mm) outside the edges of each central knot, and outside the straight lines of the border; these lines anchor the quilt top solidly to the backing and give just a little bit of extra definition to the pattern. Remove any pins or tacking stitches.

7 All the way round the quilt edge, fold the backing fabric over the front in a double 1/2in (1cm) hem. Pin and tack the hem in place. Using yellow sewing thread, hemstitch the folded edge of the hem down to the quilt front. Remove the tacking threads.

19in (48cm) If you are using a photocopier enlarge by 215%

BIRDS SOFA THROW

*Four spectacular Celtic birds decorate this square
sofa throw, surrounded by a knotwork border.
Instead of being worked in the traditional way for
wholecloth quilting, with the quilting stitches in the
same colour as the background fabric, the lines of
this design are all stitched in coloured cotons à
broder, which produces an unusual, pastel-coloured
effect on the cream background.*

SIZE OF FINISHED DESIGN: 47in (120cm) square

MATERIALS

- ❖ *Cream cotton fabric, one piece 47in (120cm)
  square and one piece 50in (127cm) square*
- ❖ *2oz wadding, 47in (120cm) square*
- ❖ *Coton à broder: two skeins of cream and mid
  green, and one skein each in the following
  colours – dark green, mid purple, dark purple,
  pink, yellow, mid orange, dark orange, jade
  green, mid blue, royal blue, mid aquamarine,
  dark aquamarine, scarlet and rust*
- ❖ *Water-soluble pen*
- ❖ *Medium sewing needle*
- ❖ *Cream sewing thread*
- ❖ *Tacking needle and thread*
- ❖ *Pencils, paper and black felt-tip pen for drawing
  the design*
- ❖ *Quilting frame (optional)*

PRODUCING THE DESIGN

1 Wash and press the fabric squares. Enlarge the
design on pages 30–31 to the correct size (see
page 12), and go over the lines in black felt-tip
pen to make them darker. Place the smaller
cream cotton square, right side up, over the
design and pin it in position so that there is an
equal border of fabric all round the edges of the
pattern. Trace the lines of the design onto the
fabric using a water-soluble pen.

2 Lay the larger backing square on a flat surface,
and lay the wadding on top so that there is an
equal border of fabric all around the wadding
square. Position the marked cream fabric, right

side up, on top of the wadding and smooth the
layers so that they are all totally flat. Pin the
three layers together, then tack them with an
even grid of horizontal and vertical lines of
tacking about 2–3in (5–7.5cm) apart (see page
14). Remove the pins.

3 Using the colours of coton à broder marked on
the design, and working with a quilting hoop or
frame if you wish (see page 12), begin quilting
around the lines of the design using small, even
quilting stitches (see page 15). Begin with the
two green knots near the centre and work
outwards, completing all the birds before
working on the border. When you come to the
border, stitch the inside straight edges first, then
the knotwork and the corner decorations, then
the outside straight edges. When all the lines of
the design are complete, remove the tacking
threads from the work.

4 Lay the design on a surface that will not cause
running or staining (eg, a clean Formica worktop
or a clean towel) and spray it all over with cold
water to remove the marks left by the water-
soluble pen. Leave to dry completely. If any pen
marks remain, simply spray the design again
and leave to dry.

5 All the way round the quilt edge, fold the
backing fabric over the front in a double ³/4in
(2cm) hem. Pin and tack the hem in place. Using
cream sewing thread, hemstitch the folded edge
of the hem down to the quilt front, or secure it
with a small zigzag machine stitch.

PRACTICAL TIPS

- ✧ *This is an excellent project for using up scraps of
  thread you have left from other projects. Don't
  feel confined into using the colours specified –
  mix and match them as you wish!*
- ✧ *Dressmakers' tracing paper comes in large
  sheets and is useful for drawing up large designs
  such as this one.*
- ✧ *To help you position the design accurately, fold
  the fabric in half diagonally first.*

✧ KEY ✧

A cream
B mid green
C dark green
D mid purple
E dark purple
F pink
G yellow
H mid orange
I dark orange
J jade green
K mid blue
L royal blue
M mid aquamarine
N dark aquamarine
O scarlet
P rust

◈ VARIATIONS ◈
These birds can be worked larger still and used to decorate a double bed quilt; for a more traditional feel, stitch them in white on a white background. Alternatively, use bright-coloured fabrics for each section of the birds and produce them in stained glass patchwork like the appliqué birds on page 48.

45in (114.5cm)

APPLIQUE

There are many different methods of appliqué used by stitchers across the world – and just about all of them can be adapted to Celtic work! As we have seen, Celtic designs are so varied in size, approach and complexity, that it is easy to find one to suit your favourite appliqué technique.

BIAS BINDING APPLIQUE

If you are new to appliqué, one of the easiest ways to achieve a Celtic look is simply to weave a long strip of bias binding (plain or print) into a simple Celtic knot on the surface of a square of fabric. The edges are then stitched down by hand or machine. You can see this technique illustrated in Fig A. As you grow more confident, you can make the knots larger and more complex. Virtually any knot design can be reproduced using this technique. You can make up your own designs too by experimenting with where the bias strip falls on the fabric.

STAINED GLASS PATCHWORK

A slight variation on this, is the technique known as stained glass patchwork. It is called patchwork because different fabrics are used, but it is really a method of appliqué. None of the patches are pieced, they are simply cut to shape and laid side by side like the pieces of a jigsaw puzzle. The raw edges are then covered and sealed with strips of stitched bias binding. As you will see from Fig B, the strips of bias binding are applied in order so

The knot design on this silk cushion was created with a sewing machine

that they conceal the raw edges of previous strips. The bird wall hanging on page 48 is produced using this method of appliqué. Because there is no piecing it is a very quick method, and can achieve spectacular results in a surprisingly short time! Many Celtic designs work well in this technique, particularly animal and geometric designs, but if the design is complex you will need to work it on a large scale otherwise it becomes too fiddly to apply the bias binding. For stained glass patchwork and for the bias binding method, the bias binding can be bought or handmade. Cotton or cotton/polyester fabrics work well and hold their shape firmly, but the satin bias bindings on the market also look good for special finishes and can give a metallic sheen to the work.

HAND-STITCHED APPLIQUE

If you are competent at appliqué and favour hand-stitching such as Baltimore appliqué you will find this a good technique for adapting some of the more complex animal and bird designs. In Baltimore appliqué, shapes are cut from different fabrics, their edges turned under and then applied

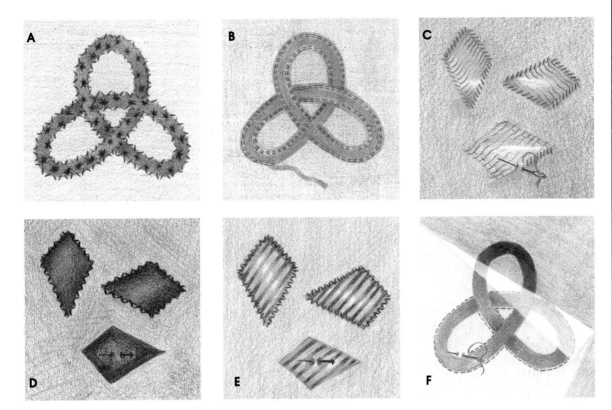

individually to the background (see Fig C) to build up designs. Folk-art appliqué also works well with Celtic designs. In this technique brightly coloured shapes are cut from felt or other non-fray fabrics and are then applied with bold running stitches in contrasting colours – the stitching is considered part of the design.

MACHINE APPLIQUE

Machine appliqué is growing in popularity as more and more sewing machines on the market do a good satin stitch or close zigzag. Doing your appliqué by machine is no longer thought of as cheating! The wonderful ranges of machine-embroidery threads developed in recent years also help; high-quality threads are now available in many colours, including space-dyed versions, and the improvement in metallic threads means that they are now much easier to use in the machine.

Machine appliqué can take several forms. The basic divisions are: using straight stitch or zigzag to appliqué shapes which have been cut and had the raw edges turned under; applying non-fray fabrics such as felt and jersey with zigzag, when the raw edges do not need to be turned under (see Fig D), and using machine satin stitch or close zigzag to enclose the raw edges of the fabrics (see Fig E). The ring cushion on page 34 and the dragon picture on page 40 use the final method, showing how the same technique can look totally different depending on the design; for this method it's also helpful to use a temporary backing such as Stitch 'n' Tear to avoid distorting the fabric.

SHADOW QUILTING

One unusual method of appliqué is shadow quilting. This involves cutting shapes from bright or dark fabrics, laying them in position on a background, then covering the top with a layer of translucent fabric such as organdie or muslin. The layers are then stitched through around the edges of the shapes to produce a subtle, muted design (see Fig F). The cot quilt on page 44 is worked in shadow quilting.

WEDDING RING CUSHION

Continuous Celtic knots are used to signify eternity, so they are perfect for showing the love of a married couple. This wedding ring cushion is beautiful and delicate, but surprisingly easy to make. It could be carried by a bridesmaid, flower girl or pageboy, or kept at the front of the church as the wedding party comes in. The cushion is made in two colours of silk, ivory and pink, to add a touch of luxury.

SIZE OF FINISHED CUSHION: 14in (36cm) square

MATERIALS

- ❖ *Pink silk, 16in (40cm) square*
- ❖ *White or ivory silk, 16in (40cm) square*
- ❖ *Muslin, 16in (40cm) square*
- ❖ *Firm white backing fabric, 16in (40cm) square*
- ❖ *2oz wadding, 16in (40cm) square*
- ❖ *Bias strip of pink silk, 60 x 2in (1.5m x 5cm)*
- ❖ *Medium piping cord, 60in (1.5m)*
- ❖ *Synthetic stuffing*
- ❖ *Pink machine embroidery thread to match the pink silk*
- ❖ *White sewing thread*
- ❖ *Double-sided iron-on bonding web*
- ❖ *Pencil and paper for drawing the design*
- ❖ *Fading pen*

PRODUCING THE DESIGN

1   Enlarge the design on page 36 to the correct size (see page 12). Lay the bonding web, paper side up, over the drawing and trace the lines onto the paper. Cut out the shape roughly, leaving a small margin outside the lines.

2   Press the square of pink silk. Lay it right side down on a flat surface and lay the bonding web on top, paper side up. Pin the two layers together in a couple of places so that they don't move during fusing. Press with a warm iron to fuse the web onto the back of the fabric. Cut out around the solid lines only.

3   Press the square of white or ivory silk, and lay it right side up on a flat surface. Peel the backing paper away from the bonding web on the knot design and position the knot in the centre of the background silk square so that there is an even border on all four edges. When you are happy with the positioning, press the design with a warm iron to fuse it to the background. Using the fading pen, mark on the front of the design where the lines of the knot overlap. Remember that the overlapping of the knot in the design is reversed so refer to the photograph to check how the design works.

4   Lay the square of muslin on a flat surface and cover with the square of wadding. Lay the square of silk, right side up, on top of the wadding, and

smooth the layers to make sure that they are flat. Pin and tack the three layers together with a grid of horizontal and vertical lines of tacking at regular intervals (see page 14).

5   Thread your sewing machine with the pink thread and set it to a medium-width satin stitch (about 2–2.5mm). Stitch around all the lines of the design, following the lines of the knot. Try to secure the end of each line of stitching under a subsequent stitching line. Where this is not possible, work a few reverse stitches at the end of the line. When all the stitching is complete, remove the tacking threads.

6   Fold the bias strip over the piping cord, right side out, and stitch close to the cord using a zipper or piping foot. Lay the cushion front on a flat surface, right side up, and lay the piping round the edges, raw edges to the outside. Pin and tack 1/2in (1.25cm) from the raw edges, rounding the corners of the square slightly. Stitch around this line by machine as close to the piping cord as possible, using a zipper or piping foot.

7   Lay the square of backing fabric on top of the cushion front, right sides together, and pin and tack along the same stitching line. Stitch round the edges again by machine, leaving about 6in (15cm) unstitched for turning out.

8   Trim the edges to within 1/4in (5mm) of the seam and clip the corners. Turn the cushion right side out and press just the edges very gently, making sure that you don't compress the piping. Stuff the cushion lightly so that it is pleasantly padded but not over-full, then close the gap using slipstitch or ladder stitch (see page 13).

PRACTICAL TIPS

- ✧ *If you are entrusting the real rings to a small attendant at the wedding, stitch two toning silk ribbons in the centre of the cushion. Tie the rings in position, using bows so that the ribbons can be undone at the crucial point in the service.*
- ✧ *Using a fading pen means that you don't need to make any permanent marks in the silk. The marks will disappear in about 72 hours, though, so if you plan to work more slowly, use a water-soluble pen and remove the marks with a dab of cold water when the design is finished.*

11in (28cm)

If you are using a photocopier enlarge by 175%

✧ VARIATIONS ✧

Many other circular, continuous knots work well
for wedding items such as the ring cushion – try
one of the designs on page 108 as an alternative.
Another way of working the pattern shown is as
a single-colour wholecloth or corded quilting
design instead of appliqué.

SPARKLING EVENING BAG

The metallic fabrics and fake gemstones on this evening bag make it look like the jewel-encrusted cover of an illuminated manuscript. The sheen and the vivid colours of the metallic fabrics are enhanced by outlines of black machine satin stitch, which quilt the design at the same time as appliquéing the fabric shapes. Use the colours shown here, or use up metallic scraps in other colours.

SIZE OF FINISHED BAG 10 x 12¹/₂in (25 x 32cm)

MATERIALS

❖ Firm black fabric, two pieces each 30 x 14in (76 x 36cm)
❖ Gold metallic fabric, at least 11 x 9in (28 x 23cm)
❖ Large scraps of metallic fabric in purple, scarlet, royal blue and emerald green
❖ Double-sided iron-on bonding web, 11 x 9in (28 x 23cm)
❖ Dolmette or similar thin padding or wadding, 30 x 14in (76 x 36cm)
❖ Imitation gemstones – 4 green square jewels, 8 circular royal blue jewels, 24 gold droplets
❖ One reel of black machine embroidery thread (cotton or rayon)
❖ Stitch 'n' Tear, 11 x 9in (28 x 23cm)
❖ Tacking thread and needle
❖ Reel of invisible thread
❖ Dressmakers' carbon paper and pencil
❖ Clasp or closure for the bag (optional)

PRODUCING THE DESIGN

1 Wash and press the pieces of black fabric. Enlarge the design opposite to the correct size (see page 12), and trace it onto the paper side of the iron-on bonding web. Mark the traced areas with the colours as specified on the design, then cut around the lines of the design, leaving a small margin outside the shapes where possible (this will not be possible with the small internal red and green squares).

2 Iron the bonding web shapes onto the backs of the appropriate metallic fabrics, then cut out the fabric shapes along the marked lines.

3 Measure in 2in (5cm) from one short edge on one of the black fabric pieces, and tack across the measured line. Pin the dressmakers' carbon paper to the front of the fabric, carbon side down, and lay the enlarged design over it so that one long edge aligns with the tacked line. Go over the lines of the design lightly with a pencil so that they are transferred to the fabric. Remove the carbon paper and the tacking thread from the fabric.

4 Peel the backing paper off the large gold appliqué pieces and put them in position, face up, on the black fabric, fusing them carefully in

place with a warm iron. Fuse the other metallic fabric pieces into position in the same way.

5 Lay the rectangle of dolmette on a flat surface and cover it with the decorated black fabric, right side up. Tack the two layers together along the edges. Position the Stitch 'n' Tear rectangle under the appliquéd design and tack all three layers together between the sections of the design. The Stitch 'n' Tear will provide extra support beneath the stitching area.

6 Set your sewing machine to a 3mm satin stitch and stitch round the inside two edges of the corner red squares and the inside three edges of the small green squares. Then go round all the other lines of the design, making sure that the lines are as straight as possible and the corners crisp. Remove the remains of the Stitch 'n' Tear from the back of the design. Lay the appliqué face down on a soft surface such as a towel and press it lightly with a warm iron.

7 Following the arrangement shown in the photograph below, use invisible thread to stitch jewels in place along the centre of each side of the design. On each central green shape, stitch four gold droplets radiating out from the central red squares.

This detail shows the radiating arrangement of the imitation jewels

10¹/2in (27cm)

If you are using a photocopier enlarge by 170%

8 Lay the two black rectangles right sides together and stitch a ¹/2in (1cm) seam around three edges, leaving the short end opposite the appliqué open for turning. Clip the corners, trim the seam allowances and turn the shape to the right side, then press the edges. Fold the raw edges of the opening inwards ¹/2in (1cm) and tack them together. Topstitch the gap closed and press.

9 Fold the bottom end of the bag inwards by 8in (20cm) and press then pin into position. Topstitch ¹/4in (5mm) in from the edge around all the sides of the new rectangle formed – along the bottom of the bag, up the edges, and across the edge of the flap. Fold the flap over to create an even border at the top and bottom of the appliqué, then topstitch along the fold to make it firm. Add a clasp or closure if you wish.

PRACTICAL TIP
✧ *For a stiffer bag, slip a layer of pelmet-weight Vilene inside the bag after you've turn it out and before you close the opening.*

✧ VARIATION ✧

For an evening bag to go with pastel colours, use silks on a gold-and-white fabric background. This would also work well with white or ivory silk for a bridal handbag.

DRAGON PICTURE

Celtic art sometimes features creatures that are a cross between dragons and reptiles; this dragon picture is developed from a design of this kind found on the ends of a Celtic casket. The design is created from unusual fabrics to emphasise the exotic nature of the animal. Don't worry about imitating them exactly, but choose your own unusual scraps of silk, shot or metallic fabrics.

SIZE OF FINISHED DESIGN: 16 x 11in (41 x 28cm)

MATERIALS

❖ *Blue/purple shot or patterned fabric, at least 15 x 8in (38 x 20cm)*
❖ *Scraps of five other toning shot or metallic fabrics*
❖ *Firm white or cream textured background fabric, 20 x 14in (51 x 36cm)*
❖ *Two reels of black Madeira rayon machine embroidery thread*
❖ *Double-sided iron-on bonding web, 18 x 12in (46 x 30.5cm)*
❖ *2oz wadding, 20 x 14in (51 x 36cm)*
❖ *Tacking needle and thread*
❖ *Pencil, paper and black felt-tip pen for drawing the designs*
❖ *Frame or mount with an aperture to fit the finished design*

PRODUCING THE DESIGN

1 Enlarge the two dragon shapes on pages 42 and 43 to the correct size. Go over the lines of dragon A with black felt-tip pen to make them darker. Press the background fabric and lay it over the dragon A drawing so that there is a roughly even border of fabric at the sides, top and bottom. Pin the fabric to the paper so that it doesn't move during tracing, and trace the lines in pencil onto the fabric. Remove the pins from the work.

2 Draw the reverse dragon shape, dragon B, onto the paper side of the bonding web, and mark the sections with the letters specified. Cut out the shapes along the marked lines. Press the

appliqué fabrics. Choose which ones will be used for which parts of the dragon, and fuse the appropriate pieces of bonding web onto the back of each fabric with a moderate iron.

3 Cut out the fabric shapes along the edges of the bonding web pieces and lay them in position on the drawing on the background fabric to check that you have cut all the pieces correctly and that you are happy with the way they look together. Remove the backing papers from the fabric pieces and fuse them into position one by one – begin with the large body and wing pieces, then add the smaller pieces in turn. Press the whole design once it is assembled.

4 Lay the design over the rectangle of wadding and pin in position. Tack through the two layers to hold them together and then remove the pins from the work.

5 Thread your sewing machine with the black thread, and select a 4mm satin stitch. Stitch across the internal lines of the design first – for instance, the central line and cross-bars of the wing, the scallops along the dragon's body – before you stitch the outer lines. This way, the ends of the first lines of stitching are secured under later lines. When the stitching is complete, remove the tacking threads.

6 Mount the picture in your chosen frame, stretching it gently over the backing board to remove any wrinkles in the fabric.

PRACTICAL TIPS

✧ *If you find it difficult to produce an even satin stitch on your machine, check your bobbin carrier. If it has a small hole at the end of the arm, thread the bobbin thread through the hole before you load the carrier in the machine – this will make your satin stitch more regular.*

✧ *You may also find it helpful to put an extra support layer underneath the stitching area. Use a rectangle of Stitch 'n' Tear, or a piece of typing paper, then tear away the excess when you have finished all the stitching.*

DRAGON A

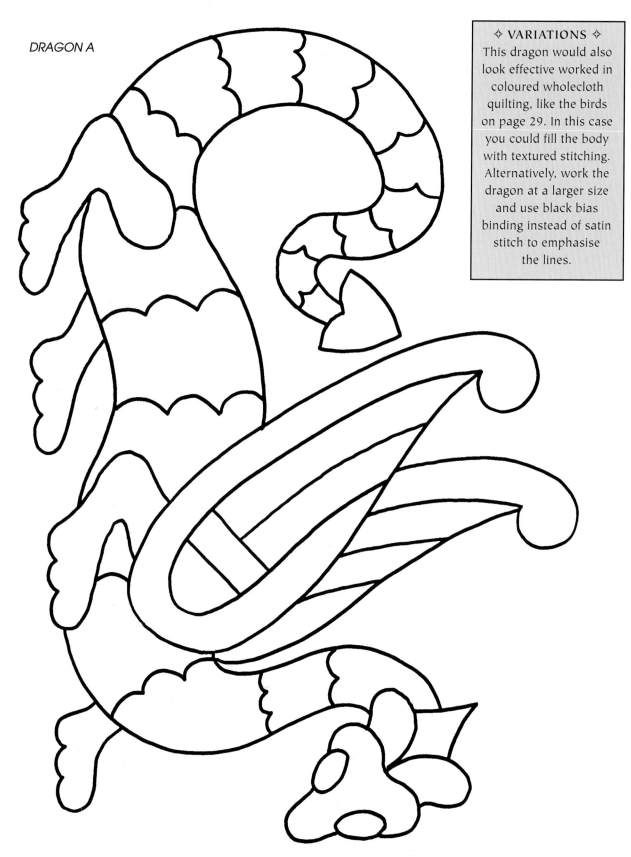

✧ VARIATIONS ✧

This dragon would also look effective worked in coloured wholecloth quilting, like the birds on page 29. In this case you could fill the body with textured stitching. Alternatively, work the dragon at a larger size and use black bias binding instead of satin stitch to emphasise the lines.

DRAGON B

16in (40.5cm)

If you are using a
photocopier enlarge
by 185%

SHADOW-WORK COT QUILT

Shadow quilting is used for this very pretty knotwork cot quilt. The shapes are cut from mid-pastel fabrics and enclosed under a layer of organza. The quilt is padded with wadding, then the lines of the knots are stitched round by hand to emphasise the shapes and to quilt the design.

SIZE OF FINISHED QUILT: 35 x 45in (90 x 115cm)

MATERIALS

❖ *White cotton fabric, 35 x 45in (90 x 115cm)*
❖ *Crystal organza, 35 x 45in (90 x 115cm)*
❖ *Mid-pastel fabrics, all at least 36in (90cm) wide, in the following colours and lengths – aquamarine ¹/₄yd (25cm); pink ¹/₂yd (45cm); green ¹/₄yd (25cm); buttercup yellow ¹/₄yd (25cm); mauve ¹/₄yd (25cm); scraps of orange*

- ❖ *Cotton or cotton/polyester backing fabric in a toning colour, 38 x 48in (97 x 122cm)*
- ❖ *2oz wadding, 35 x 45in (90 x 115cm)*
- ❖ *Quilting threads in the following colours – aquamarine, pink, green, buttercup yellow, mauve and orange*
- ❖ *Stitching thread to match the backing fabric*
- ❖ *Tacking thread and needle*
- ❖ *Medium sewing or quilting needle*
- ❖ *Thick paper*
- ❖ *Pencils and paper for drawing the pattern*

PRODUCING THE DESIGN

1 Using thick paper, enlarge the individual knot designs and the circle on page 46 to the correct size (see page 12), and cut them out.

2 Use the triangular-shaped knot as a template to cut out two shapes from the buttercup yellow fabric, two from the mauve fabric and four from the green fabric. You may find it easier to draw around the shapes on the fabric in pencil or crayon first.

Use the corner knot to cut out four shapes from the aquamarine fabric.

Use the central rectangular knot to cut one large shape from the pink fabric.

Use the circle template to cut four from the green fabric, four from the yellow fabric, four from the mauve fabric, six from the orange fabric, and two from the aquamarine fabric. Keep the circles as neat as possible.

3 Wash and press the white fabric, then fold it in half in both directions and press the folds. This divides the rectangle into quarters and will make it easier to position the coloured shapes correctly. Following the design on page 47, lay the shapes in the correct arrangement on the white background, making sure that the design is symmetrical horizontally and vertically. Pin the shapes into position, but put the pins in from the back of the work so that you can remove them easily later.

4 Press the piece of organza and lay it over the front of the design so that it encloses the coloured shapes. Tack carefully outside the edges and across the knot shapes, securing each one so that it cannot move out of position. Also

stitch some lines of tacking vertically and horizontally across the quilt top. When the organza is firmly in place, remove the pins, then press the whole design from the back to remove the fold marks.

5 Lay the backing fabric right side down on a flat surface and position the wadding on top so that there is an even border of fabric all round the edges. Lay the quilt top, right side up, on top of the wadding and make sure that all the layers are smooth. Pin the layers into position, then tack them with a grid of horizontal and vertical lines of tacking at regular intervals across the quilt. Remove the pins.

6 Thread your needle with pink quilting thread and, beginning at the centre of the large pink knot, quilt along the edges of the design and across it where the lines interweave. Refer to the design to show you which lines cross over which – if you remember that the line of each knot goes alternately over and under the ones it meets you will soon get into the rhythm! When the pink knot is complete, use yellow to quilt the yellow knots in the same way. Then work the green knots, the mauve ones, and finally the aquamarine corner knots. Stitch round each circle in thread of the appropriate colour, then remove all the tacking threads.

7 Fold over a double hem of the backing fabric all round the outside of the quilt, and tack it into position over the raw edges of the quilt top. Stitch round the folded edge by hand or machine to finish the quilt.

PRACTICAL TIPS

- ✧ *You can use any relatively stable fabric to make the coloured knots – pure cotton fabrics and polyester/cotton mixes are ideal. Other fabrics such as silk and satin can also be used; in this case, back them with a lightweight iron-on bonding web before you cut them out to stop them from fraying.*
- ✧ *Choose quite a strong yellow fabric as a pale yellow will get lost against the background. Also, pick quilting threads that are several shades darker than your coloured fabrics so that the stitching defining the knotwork will show up.*

17¹/₂in (44.5cm)

If you are using a photocopier enlarge all the shapes on this page by 168%

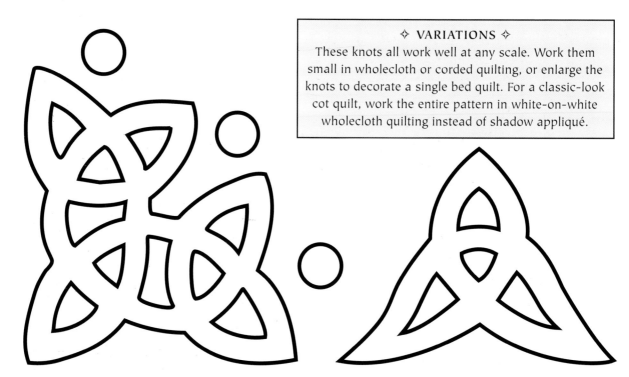

✧ VARIATIONS ✧
These knots all work well at any scale. Work them
small in wholecloth or corded quilting, or enlarge the
knots to decorate a single bed quilt. For a classic-look
cot quilt, work the entire pattern in white-on-white
wholecloth quilting instead of shadow appliqué.

STAINED-GLASS WALL HANGING

Two Celtic-style birds face each other in a classic Celtic design, interpreted this time in stained glass appliqué. The coloured sections of the design are cut from different fabrics and assembled like a jigsaw, then their raw edges are covered with strips of contrasting bias binding.

SIZE OF FINISHED HANGING: 20 x 42in (51 x 107cm)

MATERIALS

❖ *Firm cotton fabrics in the following colours and amounts:*
  pale yellow background fabric, one piece 20 x 42in (51 x 107cm), one piece 22 x 44in (56 x 112cm) (fabric A);
  plain mid grey fabric, 18in (46cm) square (fabric B);
  patterned mid yellow fabric, 14in (35cm) square (fabric C);
  patterned dark yellow fabric, 6 x 18in (15 x 46cm) (fabric D);
  patterned black and white fabric, scraps (fabric E);
  plain mid yellow fabric, scraps (fabric F);
  mid grey fabric with small dots, 16in (40cm) square (fabric G);
  patterned mid grey fabric, 6 x 14in (15 x 35cm) (fabric H);
  patterned pale grey fabric, scraps (fabric I)
❖ *Lightweight iron-on Vilene, 18 x 36in (46 x 90cm)*
❖ *16yd (15m) charcoal grey bias binding, roughly ⁵/₁₆in (8mm) wide*
❖ *Charcoal grey sewing thread*
❖ *Yellow or cream sewing thread*
❖ *2oz wadding, 20 x 42in (51 x 107cm)*
❖ *Pencils, paper and black felt-tip pen for drawing the design*

PRODUCING THE DESIGN

1 Enlarge the pattern on pages 52–53 to the correct size (see page 12), then go over the lines with black felt-tip pen to make them darker. Mark each piece of the design with the appropriate letter (refer to the fabric placement diagram on page 51).

2 Lay the piece of Vilene, smooth side up, over the drawing and trace the lines of the design onto the Vilene with black felt-tip pen – trace the letters too, lightly in pencil, for easy reference. Cut the two bird shapes out of the Vilene, cutting only along the outlines of the shapes.

3 Carefully cut one of the paper bird drawings into sections along the marked lines, and use the sections as templates to cut the appropriate fabrics, cutting two mirror-image pieces for each different shape. When all the shapes have been cut, turn the Vilene pieces over so that the slightly rough, fusible side is upwards. You should be able to see the felt-tip pen lines marked on the back. Use these to assemble the two bird shapes on the Vilene shapes, like two mirror-image jigsaw puzzles. When you are happy with the positions of all the fabrics, carefully lower a medium-hot iron onto the assembled shapes to fuse them to the bonding web – don't move the iron to and fro or you might dislodge the fabrics.

4 You now have two bird shapes with all their fabric pieces in position. Fold the smaller rectangle of pale yellow background fabric in half down its length, and position the bird shapes on this background so that they are at the same height and the same distance as each other from the central fold. Tack the shapes in position on the background, then press the fabric to remove the fold line.

5 The next stage is to add the strips of bias binding. Each strip is laid over the join between two fabric pieces and attached by stitching down first one side and then the other with a small machine zigzag stitch. The strips are added in order so that the raw ends of earlier strips are covered by subsequent strips wherever possible. Begin with the strips that go across the neck, the line across the top of each foot, the very top and very bottom straight bars of the wings, and the stripes, wavy lines and chevrons across the tail feathers. At the points of the chevrons, fold the

bias binding crisply to make a good angle. Where the lines curve, ease the bias binding to follow the shape.

6   The next lines to be done are the curved points on the wings. Shape these round the curves and fold the angles at the bottom crisply, then cover them with the inner bars across the wings. Add the strips down the centres of the beaks, and the angled sections at the tops of the beaks.

7   Next, in the same way, stitch bias binding round the edges of the large tail feathers. Leave the outside edges unstitched for about 2in (5cm) where the leg parts join, as you will need to slip in a raw edge of bias binding under these sections later. When you have done the large feathers, do the middle ones and then the small ones. Add lines around the eyes, tucking the raw edges under themselves so that they are sealed in by the stitching.

8   The final line of bias binding on each bird is a very long one, so make sure that you have single pieces of binding long enough – if you're not sure, lay them out along the line to check. Tuck the raw end of the binding under the top of the large tail feather line, then take it all round the wing, up over the back and head, round the beak, down the neck and stomach, round the foot and back up to the tail feather. Tuck the final raw end under the gap in the tail feather stitching, then go over that section of the tail feather to secure it. Lay the design face down on a soft surface and press it from the back.

9   Lay the remaining rectangle of pale yellow background fabric right side down on a flat surface and position the wadding on top so that there is an even border of fabric all round the edges. Lay the quilt top, right side up, on top of the wadding and make sure that all the layers

This detail shows the lines of bias binding concealing the raw edges of the fabric patches

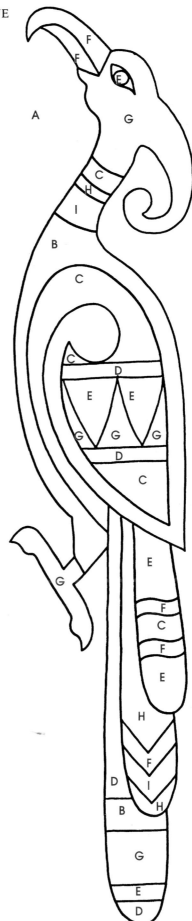

are smooth. Pin the layers into position, then tack them with a grid of horizontal and vertical lines of tacking at regular intervals across the quilt. Remove the pins.

10 Thread the sewing machine with yellow or cream thread and stitch a line of machine quilting ¹/₄in (5mm) outside each bird shape.

11 Fold over a single hem of the backing fabric all round the outside of the quilt, and tack it into position over the raw edges of the quilt top. Lay bias binding over the raw edge to conceal it and to make a frame around the hanging, then stitch the binding into place down each side. If you wish, add some hanging loops of bias binding across the top to suspend the design, or stitch a couple of buttonhole loops behind the top corners so that you can hang it invisibly.

PRACTICAL TIPS

✧ To help the bias binding to go around the curves of the design, tack each length into position first and then press it with a steam iron; the steam loosens the weave and the heat sets the curve.

✧ To obtain bias binding the correct width, buy the standard width and press one of the raw edges over further to make it slightly narrower. Alternatively, you can make your own bias binding; polyester and cotton sheeting comes in very wide widths, so allows you to make long strips of bias binding at a time. For extra speed, use a rotary cutter and board with a suitable quilting rule.

✧ KEY ✧

A pale yellow background
B plain mid grey
C patterned mid yellow
D patterned dark yellow
E patterned black & white
F plain mid yellow
G mid grey with small dots
H patterned mid grey
I patterned pale grey

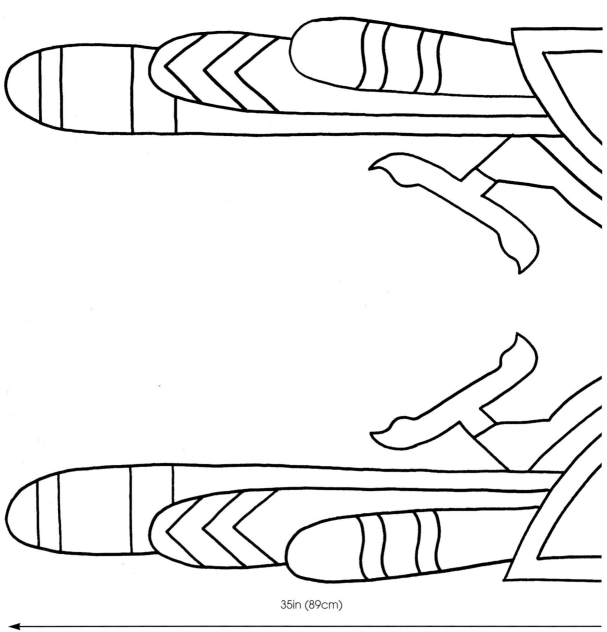

35in (89cm)

If you are using a photocopier enlarge by 380%

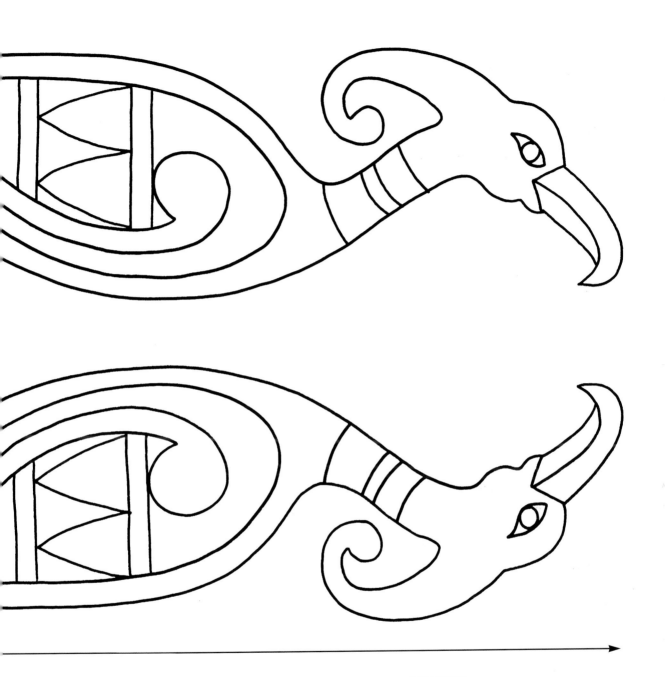

✧ VARIATIONS ✧
Any colour scheme can be used for this design.
Look through books of Celtic manuscripts for
unusual colour combinations, or substitute
fabrics that tie in with your own decor. Choose a
colour of bias binding that shows off each of the
fabrics without blending in against them.

TRAPUNTO

Trapunto literally means 'pushed through' or 'stuffed', and trapunto quilting is a method of producing patterns by stuffing just some areas of the pattern rather than by padding the entire design. There are several different methods of working trapunto quilting but the one that is used for the projects in this chapter is the technique that is also known as Italian or corded quilting, where cords or lengths of yarn are threaded through stitched channels in the design.

STITCHING CHANNELS

As you can imagine, this technique is perfect for Celtic knotwork – the continuous lines seem to have been made for corded quilting. The basic method of producing the design is the same for each project and is done in several stages. First, the top fabric is tacked to a layer of backing fabric. This backing fabric needs to be firm so that the top layer will be the one pushed out by the padding at a later stage. The lines of the design are then stitched around by hand or machine

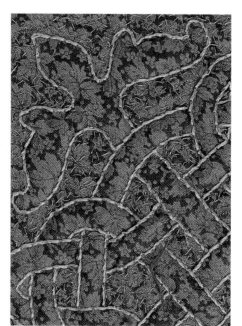

The attractive effect of trapunto

(see Fig A). If you are doing corded quilting by hand, the stitch will depend on the thread you are using. If your thread is easy to work with then you can use a fancy outline stitch such as backstitch, stem stitch or even chain stitch. The herb pillow on page 62 uses backstitch in green cotton that has then been whipped with a gold thread to make it look as though it is a twisted cord. However, if you are using a thicker or more temperamental thread, such as a metallic, then running stitch will work better. The box top design on page 68 is stitched in a gold thread

running stitch. Trapunto designs can also be stitched by machine. In this case the lines can be stitched either in straight stitch or using a narrow satin stitch. With a bit of experimentation you may also be able to stitch the channels using some of the automatic decorative stitches on your machine! The bridal handbag on page 65 is machine stitched.

PADDING CHANNELS

Once the design is stitched, the next stage is worked from the back. A bodkin or a special trapunto needle is threaded with fine cord or several lengths of yarn, then the bodkin is guided through the stitched channels, padding them with the cord or thread. If the backing fabric is very firmly woven, or if the channel to be padded is quite wide and therefore needs quite a thick thread, tiny holes are cut at the beginning and end of each channel to be threaded (see Fig B). You must do this very carefully to ensure that the front fabric is not cut. If the design is small and only needs a narrow thread to pad it, you can use a sharp-tipped bodkin and simply pierce the holes with its tip (see Fig C). When you reach a point or corner, bring the bodkin out the back of the work again and then reinsert it, leaving a small loop of the cord on the back (see Fig D). This will ensure that the cord is not pulled too tight. Where there is a larger area to be quilted, such as the letters in the initial pictures on page 58, several rows of thread are laid down side by side (see Fig E).

This method of quilting inevitably looks quite untidy on the back, so it is best for items such as pictures or box tops where the back of the work will not show. Where it might show, as in the bridal handbag, then some kind of inner lining is needed; with the handbag the silk piece is folded down to make a lining.

If you need to iron a corded quilting design once you have stuffed it, fold a clean, soft towel into several layers and place it on the ironing board. Lay the design face down on the towel and press the work gently from the back. The soft surface should ensure that the design does not get flattened.

TRAPUNTO VARIATIONS

Generally the thread or cord used for the padding does not show on the front of the work, although if your top fabric is pale it's always best to use a matching pale thread just in case the colour shows through. The initial pictures on page 58, however, use an unusual variation of trapunto. In these designs the top fabric is a sheer organza, so the padding threads are visible through it and supply the colour in the design.

Any of the knotwork designs in the other sections of the book, including the extra ones in the pattern library, can be adapted for trapunto quilting, and some spiral designs work well too. The main thing to ensure is that you have a complete channel, with stitching on both sides, for every corded part of the design. Even if a design you want to use for trapunto doesn't form channels in this way, for instance one of the key designs, you can adapt it by making every single line into a narrow double line, and threading the yarn through the channel produced while the rest of the design remains unpadded.

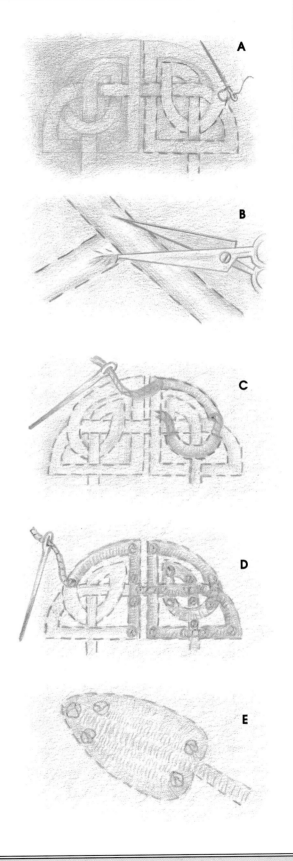

A

B

C

D

E

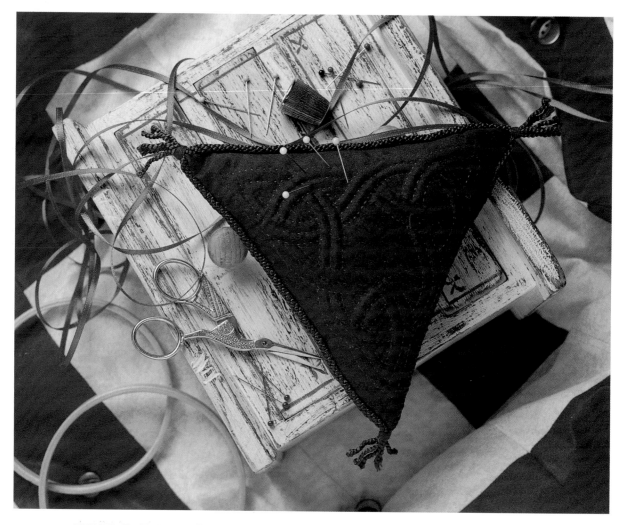

TRIANGULAR PINCUSHION

The shape of this pincushion echoes the equilateral triangle formed by the knot design on the top. This design is a double-line knot – the same line is followed by two separate channels, stitched side by side and padded individually with lengths of wool. The pincushion is made from shot navy/red silk. The red is picked out in the quilting thread and the navy in the cord used for the edging.

❖ Bodkin
❖ Medium sewing needle
❖ Red quilting thread
❖ Navy blue sewing thread
❖ 1yd (1m) blue cord
❖ Synthetic stuffing
❖ Pink crayon, slightly lighter than your red fabric
❖ Black felt-tip pen

SIZE OF THE FINISHED PINCUSHION: triangle with
7¹/₂in (19cm) sides

MATERIALS
❖ Dark red/navy shot silk, 10 x 18in (25 x 46cm)
❖ Firm backing fabric, 10in (25cm) square
❖ Skein of dark red coton à broder
❖ Skein of red tapestry wool

PRODUCING THE DESIGN
1 Press the fabrics. (You don't need to wash the silk before you use it, as you will not be laundering the finished item.) Enlarge the complete triangle design on page 57 and use the outer triangular shape as a template to cut two triangles from the silk and one from the firmer backing fabric.

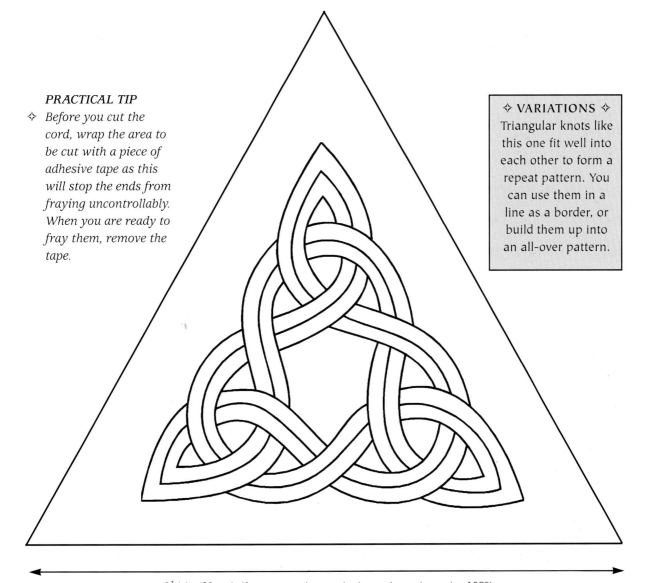

PRACTICAL TIP

✧ *Before you cut the cord, wrap the area to be cut with a piece of adhesive tape as this will stop the ends from fraying uncontrollably. When you are ready to fray them, remove the tape.*

✧ **VARIATIONS** ✧
Triangular knots like this one fit well into each other to form a repeat pattern. You can use them in a line as a border, or build them up into an all-over pattern.

8¹/4in (21cm) If you are using a photocopier enlarge by 130%

2 Trace the design, then go over the lines with a black felt-tip pen to make them darker. Lay the design on a lightbox and position one of the silk triangles, right side up, over the design so that there is an even border all round. Using the pink crayon trace the lines of the design.

3 Tack the triangle of backing fabric behind the marked triangle. Using small, even running stitches, stitch round all the lines of the knot design in the coton à broder thread. When the stitching is complete, lay the design face down on a soft surface and press. Remove the tacking.

4 To pad the channels (see page 54), use several strands of tapestry wool in the bodkin and thread both channels of the knot from the back.

5 Put the two silk triangles right sides together then pin, tack and stitch a ¹/4in (5mm) seam around the edges, leaving a small gap in one side for turning. Clip the corners and turn right side out, pressing the edges. Stuff the pincushion shape firmly, then fold under the seam allowance on the raw edges and slipstitch them closed.

6 Cut the blue cord into three even lengths. Leaving about 2in (5cm) of cord loose beyond each corner, slipstitch one piece of cord to one edge and then do the same with the other two lengths of cord along the remaining edges. At each corner of the pincushion, bind the loose ends of the cord tightly by wrapping a red sewing thread round them several times and pulling it tight. Secure the ends of the sewing thread firmly, then allow the cords to fray back to the binding at each corner to form tassels.

INITIAL PICTURES

Personalised pictures and cards are always special to the recipient. These little designs can be worked with any of the initials on the following pages, and can be used for birthday, new baby or anniversary cards, or framed as ornaments like the examples in the photograph. The technique is a combination of threaded quilting and shadow quilting – the top fabric is sheer so that the colours used for threading the design show through. The alphabet is based on Celtic uncial styles of lettering.

SIZE OF FINISHED DESIGNS: 3³/₄in (9.5cm) square

MATERIALS

(FOR THE TWO PICTURES)

- *Firm white backing fabric, two pieces each 7in (18cm) square*
- *Sheer white fabric such as organdie or crystal organza, two pieces each 7in (18cm) square*
- *Stranded cottons, one skein each in mid green, dark peach and light peach*
- *Fine gold embroidery thread*
- *Tapestry wool, one skein each in mid green, dark peach and light peach*
- *Bodkin*
- *Medium sewing needle*
- *Green and gold square frames, with an aperture roughly 4in (10cm) square*
- *Tacking thread and needle*
- *Water-soluble pen*
- *Black felt-tip pen*

PRODUCING THE DESIGNS

1   Trace or photocopy the designs on page 59. For both designs, choose your initial from the alphabet on pages 60-61. Trace your initial into the centre of the circular design, and into the top left corner of the marked square of the corner-

piece design. Go over the lines on both designs with black felt-tip pen to make them darker.

2 Lay one square of backing fabric over the first design so that there is an even border of fabric all around, and trace all the lines of the design using a water-soluble pen. Position one piece of the sheer fabric over the design, and tack the two layers together. Trace and prepare the second design in the same way using the other two pieces of fabric.

3 Using two strands of stranded cotton throughout and a small, even running stitch, stitch round the wing shapes of the circular design and the initial of the cornerpiece design in mid green. Stitch around the initial of the circular design and the fan shapes of the cornerpiece design in dark peach, and then round the circle itself and the cornerpiece knot in light peach. Finally, work a running stitch in fine gold thread about $1/8$in (2mm) outside the edge of each design.

4 When all the stitching is complete, remove the tacking threads and lay the designs on a flat surface that will not mark the fabric. Spray with cold water to remove the marks made by the water-soluble pen and leave to dry completely. If the marks do not come out fully the first time round, spray the designs again and leave to dry.

5 To pad the channels (see page 54), thread the bodkin with two or three strands of the light peach tapestry wool. Taking the needle in from the back of the work, thread the wool through the cornerpiece knot. You will need to go round the ring two or three times to fill it well. In the same way, thread the wool round the ring of the circular design. The coloured wool will show through the top sheer fabric layer.

6 Thread the bodkin with mid green tapestry wool and fill the green areas by laying down several lengths of wool side by side between the top and backing layers until each shape is well filled and slightly padded. Take the needle through to the back of the work at the end of each length, and keep checking how the work looks on the front to make sure that

you are filling the stitched pockets evenly. Finally, fill the dark peach initial with lengths of dark peach wool in the same way until it's well padded.

7 Stretch the designs over the backing pieces of the frames, making sure that both layers of fabric are completely taut. Trim away any excess fabric and assemble the frames.

For the smaller alphabet, reduce on a photocopier to 75%

HERB PILLOW

Fill this small pillow with pot-pourri or dried herbs to bring a scent of the countryside indoors even on winter days. Trapunto or corded quilting is used to make the floral knot stand out, with extra padding on the finials at the ends of the central lines. A background of seeding in fine gold thread adds extra definition. The knot design itself is formed from five separate lines twisting and crossing.

Size of finished pillow: 9in (23cm) square

MATERIALS

- ❖ Green cotton fabric with a small printed design, 10in (25cm) square
- ❖ Plain green toning backing fabric, in a firm cotton, two pieces each 10in (25cm) square
- ❖ Skein of mid-green stranded embroidery cotton to match printed fabric
- ❖ Spool of fine gold thread, eg Madeira No. 40 gold 6
- ❖ Spool of medium-thickness gold thread, eg Madeira No. 6 gold 43
- ❖ 2–3 skeins of tapestry wool
- ❖ Green sewing thread
- ❖ Tacking thread
- ❖ Medium sewing needle
- ❖ Large sharp sewing needle
- ❖ Bodkin or large tapestry needle
- ❖ Stuffing (or a mixture of stuffing and pot-pourri or dried herbs) for filling
- ❖ Skeins of extra threads to make the outside cording (coton perlé and stranded cotton in toning colours)
- ❖ Dressmakers' carbon paper or lightbox for transferring the design
- ❖ Embroidery frame (optional)

7¹/4in (18.5cm)

If you are using a photocopier enlarge by 125%

PRODUCING THE DESIGN

1 Trace or photocopy the design above. Find the centre of the green print fabric by folding it across diagonally in one direction and then in the opposite direction, pressing lightly in the centre each time. Open out the fabric and lay it right side up on a flat surface. Transfer the design onto the front of the fabric (see page 12), making sure that the design is centred accurately on the fabric with the central tips aligning and with an even border of fabric all around the pattern.

2 Lay one of the squares of backing fabric on a flat surface and place the marked square on top, right side up, so that the raw edges align. Tack the two layers together around the edges of the design, and across the centre from top to bottom and left to right.

3 Stretch the design in an embroidery frame if you wish (see page 12). Using three strands of embroidery cotton, stitch around all the lines of the design in backstitch (see page 13). Using one

63

strand of fine gold thread, work seeding stitches (see page 13) randomly to fill the spaces between the lines of the knot design. Scatter seeding stitches around the edges of the design to fill out a roughly square shape. Work the stitches slightly further apart as you move towards the outside.

4 Lay the design face down on a soft surface such as a thick towel, and press from the back with a steam iron.

5 Using one strand of the medium-thickness gold thread in the large sharp needle, bring the gold thread out at the beginning of one line of backstitch, and whip the gold through each backstitch in the same direction without catching the background fabric. This produces the effect of a fine, twisted cord. At the end of each line of backstitch, take the gold thread through to the back of the fabric and bring it up at the beginning of the next line. Complete the whole design in the same way.

6 To pad the channels (see page 54), thread the bodkin with six to eight strands of tapestry wool – you may need to experiment to see how many strands gives the best effect. At the end of each stitched channel at the back of the work, cut a small hole for the bodkin to pass through using the tip of small, sharp-pointed scissors. Be very careful not to snip the front fabric by accident. At the back of the work, take the bodkin down at the beginning of each stitched channel, thread it along the line, then bring it up at the end of each channel. Work round all the lines of the design in the same way. At points such as the corners of the knot, bring the bodkin up to the surface at the back of the work and then take it back down again. Don't pull the wool too tight, otherwise the pattern will be distorted.

7 For the floral finials at the corners of the design, lay some extra lines of wool parallel to the central line to fill out the shapes (see illustration E on page 55).

8 If the design has pulled in at all, dampen it slightly with a spray of water, then pull and pin it into shape on a stain-free pinboard, pinning along the seam allowances. Leave the work to dry completely.

9 Lay the stitched design right side up on a flat surface and lay the second green backing square over it, right side down, so that the raw edges align. Pin, tack and stitch a 1/4in (5mm) seam all the way around, leaving a 2–3in (5–7.5cm) gap along one side for turning. Clip the corners, turn the pillow right side out, and press the edges to fix the seam.

10 Stuff the pillow quite firmly with a mixture of stuffing and pot-pourri or herbs (or just stuffing if you prefer). Turn in the raw edges along the gap and slipstitch the two edges together with matching thread.

11 Make or buy 1 1/2yd (1.5m) of twisted cord for the edging. If you are making the cord, use the remains of the stranded cotton and any extra toning threads, plus one or two strands of the gold threads. Make a single overhand knot just before one end of the cord. Stitch the knot in place and wind the sewing thread tightly round the ends of the cord threads so that they cannot unravel, then cut off any raw ends. Beginning at one corner of the pillow, stitch the knot to the corner of the fabric so that any ends are hidden at the back. Continue stitching the cord along one side of the pillow until you reach the next corner, then make another knot and stitch it in position. Continue in the same way until you reach the starting point. Secure the ends of the cord very neatly at the back, then cut off any excess close to the fabric.

PRACTICAL TIP

✧ *When you are using the gold threads, only use very short lengths in your needle as the thread begins to shred when it passes through the fabric too many times, and you will waste a lot if you try and use longer lengths.*

✧ VARIATIONS ✧

This floral knot is effective worked on square designs of any size, and of course it does not have to be worked in corded quilting. Try it on square wholecloth blocks for a bed quilt, or worked in wadded silk or jacquard for an elegant scatter cushion.

BRIDAL HANDBAG

Every bride needs an elegant little bag to tuck away those essential bits and pieces on the big day. This one can be made from the same fabric as the wedding dress, or to match a bought dress. The knotwork border is stitched in gold, which can be done by hand or machine, and is then threaded with wool to pad it gently.

SIZE OF FINISHED BAG: height 12in (30cm), circumference 19in (48.5cm)

MATERIALS
- ❖ ³/₄yd (70cm) white or ivory silk, at least 36in (90cm) wide
- ❖ Backing strip of white cotton fabric, 6 x 20in (15 x 51cm)
- ❖ One reel of gold machine embroidery thread, eg Madeira metallic No. 40 gold 4
- ❖ White or cream sewing thread
- ❖ 50in (130cm) white or ivory cord for making the drawstring fastening
- ❖ Stiff cardboard, at least 13 x 6¹/₂in (33 x 17cm)
- ❖ Ball of white or cream double-knitting wool for padding the design
- ❖ Bodkin
- ❖ Pale yellow crayon or a fading pen
- ❖ Black felt-tip pen
- ❖ Craft glue

PRODUCING THE DESIGN

1 From the card, cut two circles 6in (15cm) in diameter. From the silk fabric cut one rectangle measuring 27 x 20in (68 x 51cm), two circles 7^1/$_2$in (19cm) in diameter, and two strips 1^1/$_2$ x 9in (4 x 23cm).

2 Enlarge the border design below to the correct size (see page 12), and go over the lines with black felt-tip pen to make them darker. Position one short side of the silk rectangle, right side up, over the design so that the bottom edge of the knotwork border is 2^3/$_4$in (7cm) up from the raw edge of the fabric, and so that there is an even border of fabric at each end. Trace the lines of the design onto the silk with a pale yellow crayon or a fading pen.

3 Position the strip of white cotton fabric behind the marked design, and tack the two layers together. Thread your sewing machine with gold thread in the top and white or cream thread in the bobbin. Using machine straight stitch, stitch along all the parts of the design. At the beginning and end of each stitched section, leave a loose end of the gold thread about 3in (7.5cm) long, then when the stitching is complete, pull all these threads through to the back and knot them firmly to stop the stitching from unravelling. If you have used a fading pen, leave the work for

twenty-four hours and make sure that the marks have disappeared before you pad the design.

4 Lay the design face down on a soft surface such as a clean towel and press gently on the wrong side. Remove the tacking threads. Thread the bodkin with three to four strands of wool (depending on how firmly padded you want the pattern to be) and follow the technique on page 54 to stuff the knot design, following the lines of the design as they go over and under each other. Stuff the outside border in the same way.

5 Check the width of the fabric rectangle (the edge parallel to the design) to ensure that it goes neatly round one cardboard circle with a 1in (2.4cm) overlap. If it is a bit larger, trim each end of the silk slightly; if it is smaller, either trim the cardboard circles very slightly or take a smaller seam allowance at the next stage. Fold the silk in half, right sides together, so that the long edges match, and stitch a ^{1}/$_2$in (1.2cm) seam. Press the seam open.

6 Turn the fabric tube right side out and fold the top half inwards on the dotted line indicated to make the bag lining. Using the gold thread, topstitch along the fold ^{1}/$_8$in (2mm) in from the edge. Press under ^{1}/$_4$in (5mm) along the top and bottom of each small silk strip, then fold each end under ^{1}/$_2$in (1.2cm) and stitch with the gold

17^3/$_4$in (45cm) If you are using a photocopier enlarge by 130%

thread. Pin and tack one strip on the back of the bag ie, centred over the centre back seam, and one on the front of the bag, positioning them 2in (5cm) from the topstitched edge. Stitch in gold along the top and bottom edges of each strip and then remove tacking threads.

7 Clip the seam allowance of each silk circle. Place one cardboard circle in the centre of one silk circle, on the wrong side of the fabric, and glue the clipped edges of the silk over the cardboard. Don't allow any glue to get onto the other side of the cardboard circle, otherwise it will come through the silk and mark it. Glue the other silk circle to the other cardboard circle in exactly the same way.

8 Run a gathering thread round the bottom of the raw edges of the bag, about $1/2$in (1.2cm) from the raw edges. Turn the bag shape inside out and slip one card circle $1/2$in (1.2cm) inside the bottom of the tube so that the glued side of the cardboard faces outwards. Pull the gathering thread gently so that the seam allowance is gathered onto the cardboard. Spread the inside of the second circle with glue, and carefully stick it to the first circle, trapping the seam allowance of the bag between the discs. Allow the glue to dry thoroughly after this stage before you go on to complete the bag.

9 Turn the bag right side out, and slipstitch the edges of the bag bottom to the sides to neaten them. Thread your white or ivory cord through the casings in a double loop. Cut off any excess and tie the ends. Pull up the loops at each side to close the bag.

PRACTICAL TIPS

✧ *If you prefer to stitch the design by hand, use a fine gold thread and work the design outlines in a tiny running stitch – the thread will tend to tangle too much if you use backstitch.*

✧ *To make the cord easier to thread, cut it slightly longer than you need and wrap one end in adhesive tape. This will make it firm and you can then thread it through the casing like a bodkin.*

✧ **VARIATIONS** ✧

This design can be worked in silk of any colour to produce an evening bag to match a particular gown. The design also works well at any scale in wholecloth quilting, for instance as a border for a bed quilt, or in coloured sashiko for a pair of straight curtain tie-backs.

KNOTWORK TRINKET BOX

The unusual square knot on the top of this box is formed from four identical triangular sections linked by wiggly lines. The design is stitched in gold running stitch on a plain red background. You can make up your own box, as the instructions describe, or you can work the design to fit into the top of a commercial jewellery box (adjusting the materials required accordingly).

SIZE OF FINISHED BOX: 6in (15cm) wide, 6in (15cm) deep, 3½in (9cm) high

NOTE: Work either in imperial or metric throughout – don't try and mix them, as they have been worked out individually to get the correct result.

MATERIALS

❖ *Plain red cotton fabric for the box top, ¼yd (25cm)*
❖ *Red and gold print cotton fabric for the box sides, ¼yd (25cm)*
❖ *Thin, firm calico, 9in (23cm) square*
❖ *Gold metallic fabric, 3½in (9cm) square (or a small gold tassel)*
❖ *2oz wadding, ¼yd (25cm)*
❖ *Gold hand-sewing thread, eg Madeira No. 6 gold 43*
❖ *Skein of red tapestry wool, or a small amount of double knitting wool*
❖ *Strong red thread, such as quilting or buttonhole thread*
❖ *Large-eyed sewing needle*
❖ *Bodkin or trapunto needle*
❖ *Fine curved sewing needle*
❖ *Thick cardboard (eg mounting board)*
❖ *PVA glue*
❖ *Dressmakers' carbon paper in pink or gold*
❖ *Pencil and paper for drawing the design*

PRODUCING THE DESIGN

1 Trace or photocopy the design on page 71 onto paper. From the plain red fabric, cut a piece 9in (23cm) square and fold it diagonally first in one direction and then the other. Press the folds lightly where they cross to mark the centre of the square, then unfold the fabric and lay it right side up on a flat surface. Cut a piece of dressmakers' carbon paper to fit the design, and pin it carbon side down in the centre of the fabric square. Position the design on top so that its centre is aligned with the centre of the fabric (put a pin through the middle of the design to check) and that the corners are on the diagonal fold marks. Go over the lines of the design with a pencil to transfer them. Remove the pins and the carbon paper.

2 Lay the red square, marked side up, on top of the calico square and tack together with a grid of horizontal and vertical lines of tacking at regular intervals (see page 14).

3 Using the gold thread and a large-eyed needle, stitch along the lines of the design with an even running stitch, making sure that the lines of stitching go 'over' and 'under' each other where they should. When the stitching is complete, remove the tacking.

4 Thread the trapunto needle or bodkin with a double length of red tapestry wool and, working from the wrong side, pad the stitched channels of the design (see page 54). Begin from one corner and work your way right round the knot design. When the padding is complete, press the work as described on page 55, making sure that you keep it square.

5 To make the box, first cut the following pieces from the thick cardboard:
Two pieces 6in (15cm) square – mark these TOP OUTSIDE and BOTTOM OUTSIDE.
Two pieces 5¾in (14.5cm) square – mark these TOP INSIDE and BOTTOM INSIDE.
Four pieces 3½ x 6in (9 x 15cm) – mark each of these SIDE OUTSIDE.
Four pieces 3¼ x 5¾in (8.5 x 14.5cm) – mark each of these SIDE INSIDE.

6 Arrange the four SIDE OUTSIDE pieces as in Fig 1 on page 70, and use a small amount of the PVA

glue to stick small rectangles of red fabric (each 1½ x 3in or 4 x 8cm) between them as shown to act as hinges.

7 Cut a piece of wadding to fit this new long outside piece, and separate pieces of wadding to fit each of the other remaining pieces. The only section that does not need wadding is the piece marked BOTTOM OUTSIDE. Use a small amount of the glue to stick the wadding to the appropriate pieces of card.

8 Lay all of the pieces marked INSIDE (TOP INSIDE, BOTTOM INSIDE and four SIDE INSIDES) on the plain red fabric, and for each one cut a fabric patch 1in (2.5cm) larger all round. Place each card piece, wadding side down, onto the corresponding fabric patch and using PVA glue stick two opposite edges down over the card (see Fig 2), being careful not to get glue on the front of the card. When the glue is completely dry, cut sections out of the excess fabric as shown in Fig 3. Fold the excess fabric diagonally as you would for a parcel, then stick these edges down over the card (see Fig 4).

9 Use the same method to cut and attach a long patch from the red and gold fabric over the long SIDE OUTSIDE piece, and to cut and stick a square patch over the BOTTOM OUTSIDE piece. Trim the trapunto piece to about 8in (20cm) square, and glue it over the TOP OUTSIDE section in the same way as before.

10 To make the tab which opens the box, fold the square of metallic fabric in half and then fold the corners towards the centre (see Fig 5). To make the hinge for the lid, cut a piece of plain red fabric 8 x 3in (20 x 8cm) and turn under the ends until the piece is very slightly shorter than the box top. Fold this piece in half and press (see Fig 6). Lay the top of the box right side down and stick the tab in the centre of one side and the hinge on the opposite side (see Fig 7). Now take the TOP INSIDE piece and stick it over the back of the TOP OUTSIDE piece (see Fig 8), enclosing the edges of the hinge and the tab. Make up the bottom of the box by sticking the INSIDE BOTTOM to the wrong (card) side of the OUTSIDE BOTTOM.

11 Lay the box top, right side down, on a flat surface. Take the long SIDE OUTSIDE piece and lay it, right side down, below the hinge side of the box top. Stick the other flap of the hinge to it (see Fig 9). Now stick the four SIDE INSIDE pieces in position on top of the SIDE OUTSIDE sections (see Fig 10).

12 Fold the box around into a square shape. Using the curved needle and strong red quilting or buttonhole thread, use ladder stitch (see page 13) to join the sides of the box; pull the edges together as firmly as possible. When you reach the bottom edge, attach the box bottom in the same way to complete the box.

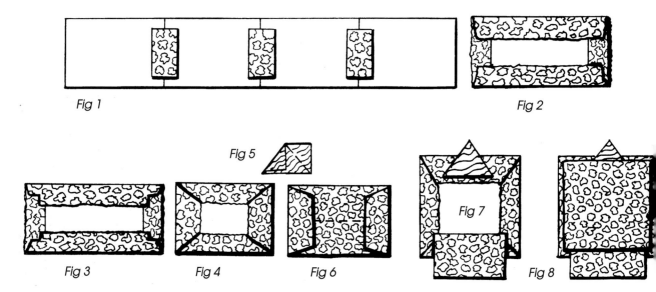

Fig 1

Fig 2

Fig 5

Fig 3

Fig 4

Fig 6

Fig 7

Fig 8

✧ VARIATIONS ✧
The square knot of this design is easily adapted to other types of quilting. Try enlarging the design on a wholecloth silk cushion, or work it in appliqué on the pocket of an evening jacket. The knot also makes a good repeat pattern for a border on a large quilt.

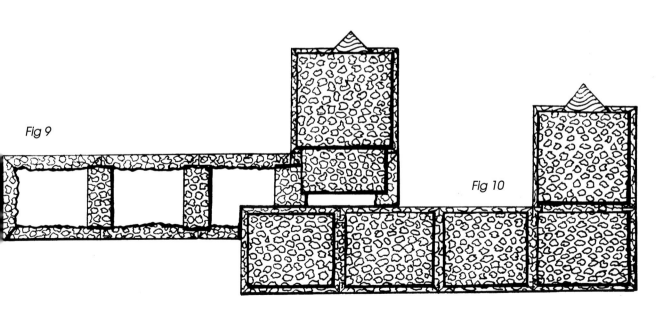

Fig 9

Fig 10

$\mathcal{P}$ATCHWORK

Patchwork, which involves joining patches of different fabrics into a decorative pattern, may not seem an obvious technique for use with Celtic designs, but it's amazing how many different types of Celtic decoration can be adapted to make patchwork designs.

The most obvious Celtic candidates to provide inspiration for patchwork are the carpet page patterns, which even if they feature knots or animals are often formed within a regular grid created from basic squares and rectangles. These grid patterns can very easily be translated into patchwork. The quilt for a child's bed on page 86 and the cushion on page 74 are both based on carpet page patterns, worked in bright patches.

Many of the Celtic key designs are also formed

Detail of a patchwork design based on a carpet-page pattern

on a regular grid of squares and rectangles, occasionally with the addition of triangles, so many of these patterns can also be re-worked as patchwork. The footstool design on page 79, pieced from squares and strips, is based on a simple square key pattern. Also, if you look behind some of the more elaborate illuminated initials and other designs in Celtic manuscripts, you'll often discover subsidiary geometric designs used as filling patterns. Once again quite a few of these lend themselves to pieced work. The strip-pieced table-mats on page 76 have been developed from one of these simple fillings.

Knotwork designs are quite a challenge to create in patchwork, but as the work-bag project on page 82 proves, it is possible! Here a striped fabric has been cut and pieced carefully in straight strips and across corners to create a knot design that really looks as though it interweaves.

ENGLISH PATCHWORK

Patchwork is generally divided into two main types: English and American. English patchwork, which is probably most familiar to stitchers in the traditional hexagon design, is pieced over papers. Each patch of fabric is tacked over a piece of paper in the required shape to stiffen it and make it easier to stitch (see Fig A). Each shape requires two templates, an inner template for the papers, and a slightly larger cutting template for the fabric. The stiffened shapes are then stitched together by hand in a tessellating pattern (see Fig B). Once the work is complete, the tacking threads are pulled out and the papers removed. English patchwork is used for shapes which cannot easily be joined with long straight or curved seams.

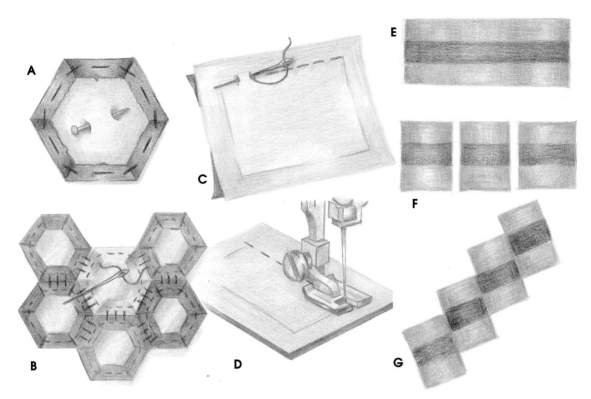

AMERICAN PATCHWORK

American patchwork does not use papers but produces patterns by seaming shaped fabric patches together in a specific order so that they form a pieced pattern. The seams are often straight, but may occasionally be curved for more elaborate designs. The stitching can be done by hand or machine. If they are being hand-stitched the patches are placed right sides together, pinned or tacked, and stitched along the seam allowance with a small running stitch (see Fig C). If they are done by machine, the patches are pinned or held together and seamed with straight stitch (see Fig D). The cushion project in this section is machine pieced by stitching a design of squares into rows, and then joining the rows. The footstool design is created by piecing a series of square patches and long strips.

STRIP-PIECING

One variation of machine piecing is strip-piecing. This involves stitching strips of fabric together in a specific sequence, then cutting this new piece of patchwork fabric into patches and re-piecing them in a different order to make a secondary design (see Figs E, F, G). The technique may sound complicated, but in fact it is very easy and is a labour-saving way of piecing all kinds of designs. The table-mats on page 76 are formed by basic strip-piecing.

PATCHWORK BASICS

Some general guidelines apply to all kinds of patchwork. Unless anything else is specified, always cut square or rectangular patches along the straight grain of the fabric so that they won't stretch or distort while being stitched. If the patches need to be cut in a different way, for instance on the bias rather than along the grain, the pattern will specify. When machine piecing, press the seams after each stitching sequence so that they lie flat and make subsequent stitching easier and neater. Generally the seams should be pressed open. The main exception to this rule is if you have one very light fabric among darker ones, in which case you may prefer to press the seams towards the darker fabric so that they don't show through on the right side.

BRIGHT CUSHION

Carpet pages and square geometric designs are
perfect for translation into simple patchwork as the
patterns can be assembled in strips and then joined
to make the whole design. This cushion, in bright
heraldic colours, is a good example of this technique.
It is made from twenty-five squares, arranged in a
simple carpet-page design, and surrounded by a
strip-and-square border. The fabrics have been cut
to emphasise their different patterns, and the whole
piece is quilted with opalescent beads that pick up
the bright colours around them.

SIZE OF FINISHED CUSHION: 20in (50cm) square

MATERIALS

❖ *Firm cotton fabric in the following colours and
sizes:*
*thirteen squares of white with a large gold motif
(fabric A), each 4in (10cm) square;*
*four squares of turquoise (fabric B), each 4in
(10cm) square;*
*eight squares of a turquoise, navy and gold print
(fabric C), each 4in (10cm) square;*

*four strips of turquoise (same as above), each
2 x 18in (5 x 46cm);*
*four squares of white with a small gold motif,
each 2in (5cm) square*
- ❖ *Muslin, 20in (50cm) square*
- ❖ *Two pieces of toning backing fabric, each
13 x 20in (33 x 50cm)*
- ❖ *2oz wadding, 20in (50cm) square*
- ❖ *20 opalescent beads*
- ❖ *White or pale turquoise sewing thread*
- ❖ *Small sewing needle*
- ❖ *Tacking needle and thread*
- ❖ *Cushion pad, 20in (50cm) square*

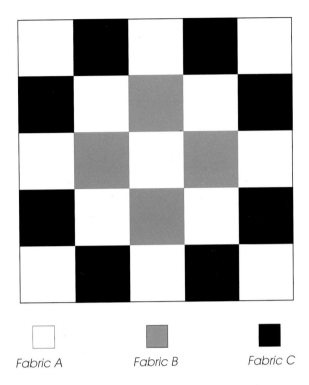

Fabric A   Fabric B   Fabric C

PRODUCING THE DESIGN

1 Wash and press the cotton fabrics. Following the piecing diagram on this page, lay the fabrics out in order on a large flat surface. Make sure that if you have a one-way design, such as the fleurs-de-lis fabric, that all the squares of that fabric are facing in the same direction. Assemble the rows first by pinning the squares of each row together in the correct order, then stitching the squares together as pinned, allowing a 1/4in (5mm) seam allowance throughout. The seams can be stitched by machine using straight stitch, or by hand using a small running stitch. Press the seams open at each stage of the assembly.

2 Lay the rows out again on a flat surface to check that you have got them in the right order and facing the right direction. Pin the rows together, then stitch them together in order, making sure that all the seams match across the design.

3 Measure the outside edges of your patchwork block (they should all be the same!) and cut the four strips of turquoise fabric to exactly that length. Stitch one strip onto the top and one to the bottom of the block. Stitch one of the smaller white squares (with the small gold motif) to the top and bottom of each remaining strip, then add these composite strips to the sides of your patchwork block.

4 Lay the square of muslin on a flat surface, then lay the square of wadding on top. Put the patchwork block right side up on top of the wadding and smooth it to make sure it lies flat. Tack the three layers together with a grid of horizontal and vertical lines of tacking, 2–3in (5–7.5cm) apart (see page 14). Stitch an opalescent bead at each intersection where four squares meet, and on the inside corner of each small white square (see photograph). Go through all three layers as you sew these on, and secure the thread firmly each time.

5 Using the toning backing fabric, turn under and stitch a small double hem on one long side of each rectangle. Lay the patchwork on a flat surface, right side up, then lay the backing rectangles on top, right sides down, overlapping them so that they make a square that aligns with the patchwork. Stitch a 1/4in (5mm) seam around the edges by machine. Clip the corners and turn the cushion cover to the right side. Press gently round the very edges only, then insert the cushion pad.

PRACTICAL TIPS
- ✧ *Only iron the very edge of the cushion cover when you have turned it out, otherwise you will flatten the wadding and lose the quilted look.*
- ✧ *Use a lightbox to help you centre the printed motifs on your cut patches.*

GEOMETRIC TABLE-MATS

The geometric key-and-step patterns used as fillings in many Celtic designs are often overlooked in favour of the more spectacular knot designs, but they can be very dramatic and effective in their own right. Like this design, they are often based on simple repeats and alternations of squares and rectangles, which makes many of the designs ideal for patchwork. These mats are produced using strip-piecing, which is a kind of patchwork production line. It's an excellent way of saving labour because you don't have to join each square and rectangle individually!

SIZE OF FINISHED DESIGN: $15^3/4$ x 8in (40 x 20.5cm)

NOTE: The measurements for cutting and piecing need to be very exact in order to make this patchwork look good. If your seams are not exact, the pieced sections will not align and the effect will be spoiled. Work either in imperial or metric throughout – don't try and mix them, as they have been worked out individually to get the correct result.

MATERIALS

FOR FOUR MATS:

❖ $^1/2$yd (50cm) cotton fabric, at least 48in (122cm) wide, in each of the following shades:
  dark blue/royal blue/gold all-over print (fabric A);
  light blue/gold all-over print (fabric B);
  yellow/white or yellow/gold all-over print (fabric C)
❖ 1yd (1m) plain royal blue cotton fabric, at least 48in (122cm) wide
❖ Yellow sewing thread
❖ Blue sewing thread
❖ Cutting mat and rotary cutter (optional)

PRODUCING THE DESIGN

1 Wash and press all the fabrics.
2 From fabric A, and using the full width of the fabric, cut one strip $4^1/2$in (12cm) wide, and two strips $2^1/2$in (7cm) wide.
   From fabric B, again using the full width of the fabric, cut one strip $4^1/2$in (12cm) wide, and two strips $2^1/2$in (7cm) wide.
   From fabric C, still using the full width of the fabric, cut one strip $4^1/2$in (12cm) wide, and four strips $2^1/2$in (7cm) wide.
3 Using a $^1/4$in (1cm) seam allowance, stitch one batch of strips together along the long edges in the following order:

fabric C narrow strip

fabric A wide strip

fabric B wide strip

fabric C wide strip

Accuracy is very important for the finished result of this project, so make sure that your seams are all exactly $^1/4$in (1cm). Some sewing machines have a special foot which will help you to stitch an exact seam. Press the seams open on the back of the work.

4 Using a $^1/4$in (1cm) seam allowance, stitch the second batch of strips (which are all narrow ones) together along the long edges in the following order:

fabric C
fabric A
fabric B
fabric C
fabric B
fabric A
fabric C.

Press the seams open on the back.

5 Now cut the pieced rectangles into strips at right angles; each strip should be $2^1/2$in (7cm) wide (see Fig 1 on page 77). Cut as many strips as you can from each rectangle.
6 The patchwork pattern is produced by re-joining these strips in different combinations to produce a secondary pattern. All the strips you have

should be the same length, whichever rectangle they were cut from. Instead of joining them so that their tops and bottoms align, each strip is joined to its neighbour by staggering it 2in (5cm) upwards. When you put the strips together you will see that this is offset by one square (or half a rectangle) each time. Following the piecing diagram (Fig 2), and using ¼in (1cm) seams, join the strips into a long band by stitching them in the order shown until you have used up all the strips containing rectangles (you will have some strips of squares left over, surplus to requirements). Press all the seams open on the back.

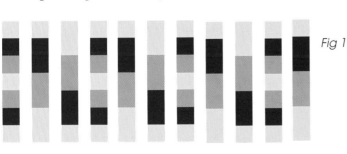

Fig 1

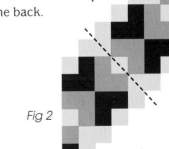

Fig 2

7 Check that the patchwork has not become distorted. If the grain is pulling more in one direction than another, spray the patchwork with spray starch, pull it into shape and iron it dry. Now cut the sections for the mats. Cut across the pieced strip as shown in Fig 2 to produce four identical sections. If you wish, trim off the tops of the staggered shapes (but do not cut right down to the seams – you still need $^1/4$in or 1cm seam allowance at the top and bottom of the strip-piecing).

8 Press the plain blue fabric. Measure your strip-pieced sections (which should all be the same size) and add 6in (13cm) in each direction. Cut four rectangles to these dimensions from the blue fabric.

9 Take one rectangle, lay it right side down on a flat surface, and fold each edge over to the front by $1^3/4$in (4.5cm). Press the folds firmly. Press under $^1/4$in (5mm) on each raw edge. Slip one of the pieced sections inside the frame produced, and check that the raw edges of the piecing are covered by the folded edges of the blue frame – if not, re-fold the edges of the blue fabric so that the border is slightly wider.

10 Remove the piecing and lay the blue fabric out flat. Fold each fabric corner at exactly 45° across the point where the border folds meet (see Fig 3), and press firmly. At each corner, place the fabric right sides together so that the border folds align, and stitch along the diagonal folds at exactly 45° to the border folds (see Fig 4), leaving the outside $^1/4$in (5mm) open. Clip the seams and press them open (see Fig 5), then turn the blue frame right side out and press, keeping the raw edges pressed under (see Fig 6). You should now have a neat frame with mitred corners which you will use to surround your section of piecing.

11 Position the pieced section inside the blue frame again, and pin and tack the turned-under edges of the frame into position round the edges of the piecing. Topstitch through all the layers using straight stitch or a narrow zigzag in blue thread. Press the finished mat.

PRACTICAL TIP

✧ *If your sewing machine does not have a $^1/4$in guide, or if you are working in metric, use the seam guides on the needle-plate.*

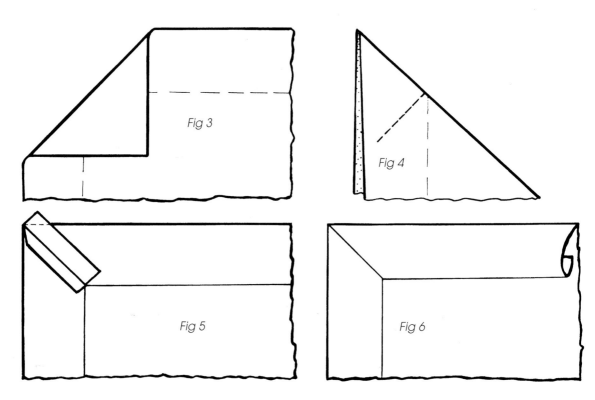

Fig 3

Fig 4

Fig 5

Fig 6

KEY-PATTERN FOOTSTOOL

The design used for this square footstool is taken from one of the square Celtic key patterns. These designs are often used as filling patterns behind more elaborate knots or illuminations and are sometimes built up into complex borders. The design is created by stitching a series of square patches and strips into a block design. All the stitching can be done by machine, which makes it a very quick design to produce.

SIZE OF FINISHED DESIGN: 13in (34cm) square
NOTE: As this design requires very accurate cutting and piecing, we have only given the metric measurements as imperial equivalents will not be accurate enough. If you prefer to work in imperial, enlarge Fig 3 on page 81 to the correct size and cut out each pattern piece separately, adding ¹/4in all round each piece for seams.

MATERIALS

❖ *Firm cotton fabrics in the following colours and quantities:*
white-on-white pattern, fat quarter metre;
red with gold pattern, fat quarter metre;
blue with silver pattern, fat quarter metre;
green with gold star pattern, scraps
❖ *Bleached calico fabric, 20cm by at least 90cm wide*
❖ *White sewing thread*
❖ *Square footstool with a 13in (34cm) pad*
❖ *Rotary cutter and board (optional)*

PRODUCING THE DESIGN

1 Wash and press all the fabrics.
2 Cut the red, white and blue fabrics into 3cm strips along the length of the rectangular pieces, and from these strips cut secondary strips in the following lengths:
  (Note: * = border strips)
  From the blue fabric, cut two strips of 31cm* and two strips of 27cm*.
  From the white fabric, cut two strips of 35cm*, two strips of 31cm*, two strips of 27cm*, two strips of 23cm*, one strip of 11cm, eight strips of 7cm, six strips of 5cm and sixteen 3cm squares.
  From the red fabric, cut two strips of 11cm, ten strips of 7cm and twenty 3cm squares.
  From the green fabric, cut four 3cm squares.
3 Ignoring the border pieces for the moment, lay out all the other pieces, right side up, according to the diagram of the central block (see Fig 1). Using a 5mm seam throughout, join all the sections of the top strip in order and when finished, press the seams open. Continue piecing each row in turn in the same way until you have eleven separate rows which you will use to create the central block.
4 Lay the rows out again in order, following the diagram, to check that they are all correct and that you have them in the right sequence. Then join the rows to each other in long, straight seams, making sure that the seams match across the rows where necessary. Press all the seams open.
5 Add the 23cm white strips to the top and bottom of the block, press the seams, then join the 27cm white strips to the sides of the block. Add the

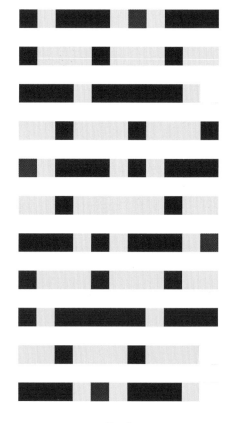

Fig 1

31cm and 27cm blue strips in the same way, following the sequence shown in Fig 2 on page 81. Finally, add the remaining 31cm and 35cm white strips to complete the design (Fig 3).
6 Add a calico border next – this gives you some extra fabric to use when stretching and securing the patchwork over the footstool. Cut two strips of calico 35 x 8cm and stitch them to the top and bottom of the finished patchwork block. Press the seams open. Cut two strips of calico 49 x 8cm and stitch them to the sides of the block. Press the seams open.
7 Follow the manufacturer's instructions for covering the pad and assembling the footstool.

PRACTICAL TIPS

✧ *If you have a hot glue gun, you may find it useful for stretching the patchwork over the footstool pad; if not, use upholsterer's tacks. Stretch and secure opposite sides first, then the remaining two sides.*

Fig 2

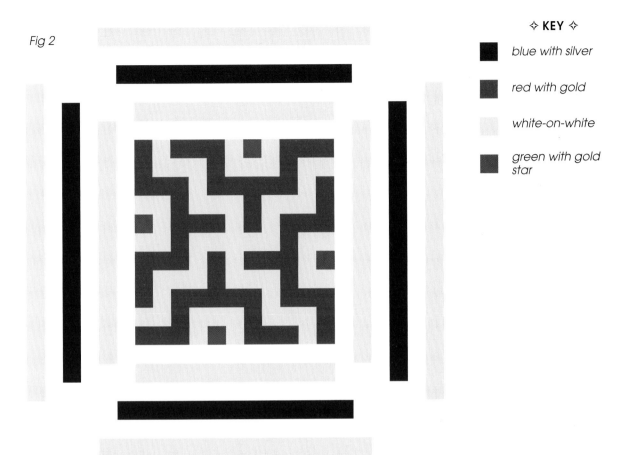

blue with silver

red with gold

white-on-white

green with gold star

✧ Although it is not essential, you will find a rotary cutter and board extremely useful for cutting the strips for this design. Lay all the fabrics on top of each other, making sure that their edges are aligned, and cut the 3cm strips. Then separate the strips and cut into the required lengths.

Fig 3

✧ VARIATIONS ✧

The square design of this footstool panel makes it perfect for cushions, or it could be worked in Christmas fabrics, padded and quilted, and used as a table-mat.

For something totally different, cut the coloured shapes on the design in a smaller size from soft leather (and without seam allowances), and appliqué them by machine onto the back of a leather jacket.

PATCHWORK WORK-BAG

The knot design on the front of this work-bag has been cleverly pieced so that it gives the illusion of an interweaving Celtic knot. The design makes use of a striped fabric, which is cut at an angle to create the corner pieces of the knot.

SIZE OF FINISHED BAG: 20in (51cm) square

MATERIALS

❖ Suitable striped fabric, 20in (51cm) long (In order to make the striped design work at this size, you will need a fabric that has a striped design about 1¹/₂in (4cm) wide, with a gap of at least 1³/₄in (4.5cm) between the stripes)
❖ Dark plain fabric to tone with striped fabric, ¹/₄yd (25cm)
❖ Pale plain fabric to tone with striped fabric, ¹/₄yd (25cm)
❖ Firm backing fabric, three 20in (51cm) squares
❖ Length of petersham for the bag handles (or use the striped fabric if you have enough)
❖ Cream sewing thread
❖ Tacking needle and thread
❖ Firm paper for inner templates
❖ Thin card for templates
❖ Pencils and paper for drawing the templates

PRODUCING THE DESIGN

1 Wash and press all the fabrics.
2 Trace or photocopy the templates on pages 84–5, and stick them all to thin card to make them more durable. (See English patchwork

page 72.) The cutting templates are for the fabrics, and the paper templates are for the inner paper shapes.

3 Using cutting template 1 (the rectangle), cut twelve pieces from the striped fabric so that the stripe is centred down the middle of the rectangle each time.

Using cutting template 2 (the square), cut twelve pieces from the striped fabric so that the stripe is centred across the middle of the square. Also use template 2 to cut thirteen square patches from the dark plain fabric.

Using cutting template 3 (the smaller triangle), cut eight patches from the light plain fabric.

Using cutting template 4 (the larger triangle), cut four patches from the light plain fabric.

4 From the remaining striped fabric, cut out two strips, each wide enough to have a stripe running down the centre with at least 1³/4in (4.5cm) extra fabric down either side. Choose the least conspicuous part of the striped pattern (in the photograph I chose one edge of the wide pink stripe in the middle) and stitch a ¹/8in (2mm) pin-tuck on the wrong side of each strip to reduce the width of the striped design. Press the pin-tuck to one side, then use template 2, at an exact 45° angle, to cut twelve square patches from these strips; cut them so that the pin-tucked stripe falls only down one triangular half of the square.

5 Use the paper templates to cut twelve papers from template 5, thirty-seven papers from template 6, eight papers from template 7, and four papers from template 8.

6 Tack the fabrics, right side out, over the appropriate papers. As the pin-tucked squares have been cut on the bias, make sure that you don't pull the edges out of shape as you tack.

7 Follow Fig 1 to assemble the pieces in the correct order. Join the pieces by putting them right sides together and over-sewing the edges that go together. Begin with the knot design and the dark square patches and make sure that you stitch the squares with the stripes in the right direction each time. Once the knot is complete, add the triangles round the edges to make the square shape.

8 When all the patches are joined, press the seams on the back so that the seam allowances all lie flat, then remove the tacking threads. Press the outside seam allowances of the square open.

9 Put the patchwork square right side together with one of the backing fabric squares and stitch with a ¹/4in (5mm) seam round three edges. Clip the corners and turn the square to the right side then press the seam. Make the other two squares up in the same way to form the other side of the bag. Put the two sides of the bag together, right sides outwards, and topstitch them together ¹/8in (2mm) in from the sides and bottom.

10 If you have any of the striped fabric left, cut two strips to the length you want the handles and fold them in half lengthways, right sides together. Stitch a small seam and turn the strips right side out and press. If you don't want to use fabric, cut two pieces of petersham to the required length.

11 Turn the seam allowances of the bag tops to the inside so that they are concealed. Pin the raw ends of the handles in position between the seam allowances, then tack along the top of each side of the bag. Topstitch along these edges, stitching ¹/8in (2mm) in from the edge.

Fig 1

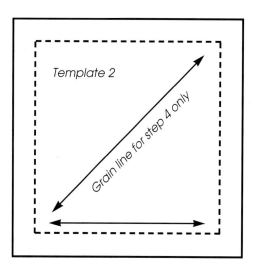

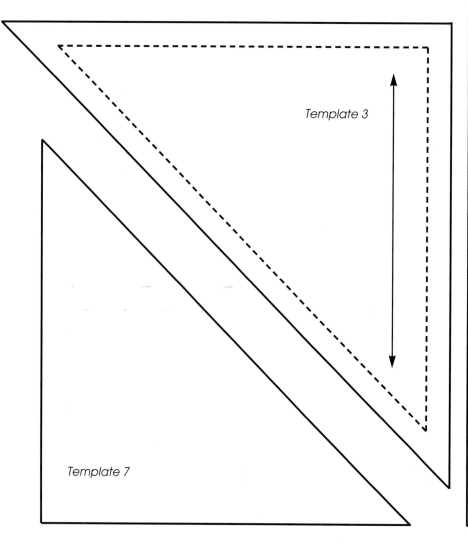

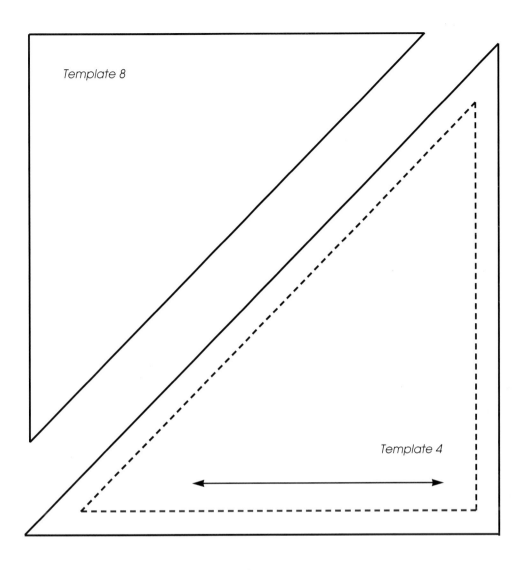

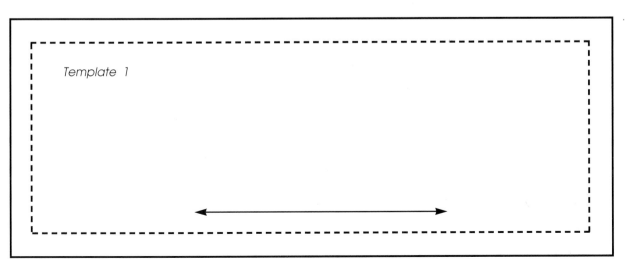

CHILD'S BED QUILT

The carpet pattern used for this bed quilt is great fun to piece and is bright and exuberant. The design may look complicated, but it is pieced very simply – strips and squares of fabric are joined into rows, then the rows are stitched together to create the patchwork pattern. Buttons in three toning colours are stitched through all the layers to quilt the design.

SIZE OF FINISHED QUILT: 76 x 58in (190 x 147cm)
NOTE: Work either in imperial or metric throughout – don't try and mix them, as they have been worked out individually to get the correct result.

MATERIALS

❖ *Firm cotton fabrics, at least 45in (114cm) wide, in the following colours and amounts:*
  pale moss green and white print, 2yd (1.8m) (fabric A);
  dark blue/purple, 1yd (90cm) (fabric B);
  mid plum, 1yd (90cm) (fabric C);
  bright pink, 1yd (90cm) (fabric D);
  mid purple small print, fat quarter yard/metre or large scraps (fabric E);
  dark plum, fat quarter yard/metre or large scraps (fabric F);
  dark moss green, fat quarter yard/metre or large scraps (fabric G);
  dark purple, fat quarter yard/metre or large scraps (fabric H)
❖ *Co-ordinating fabric to back the quilt, 2¼yd (2m), at least 60in (1.5m) wide*
❖ *2oz wadding, 76 x 58in (190 x 147cm)*
❖ *Buttons – 23 medium-sized moss-green; 48 small purple; 24 medium-sized pink*
❖ *Toning sewing thread*
❖ *Bright pink quilting thread*
❖ *Medium/large sewing needle*

PRODUCING THE DESIGN

1 Wash and press all the fabrics before you begin. If necessary, pull them diagonally so that the grain lines lie at right angles.

2 Remove the selvedges from fabric A, then cut the fabric into 3½in (9cm) strips along its length. The quilt is made up of a central panel and four borders (border 1, border 2, border 3, border 4).

FROM THE FABRIC A STRIPS CUT THE FOLLOWING:
For border 3, cut two pieces 63½in (157cm) and two pieces 45½in (116cm).
For border 1, cut two pieces 51½in (131cm) and two pieces 33½in (85cm).
For the central panel, cut six pieces 9½in (24cm), twenty-four pieces 6½in (16.5cm) and twenty pieces 3½in (9cm) square.

3 Cut all the other fabrics into 3½in (9cm) strips, cutting from selvedge to selvedge.
FROM FABRIC B CUT THE FOLLOWING:
For border 2, cut four pieces 18½in (47cm), four pieces 15½in (39.5cm) and four pieces 9½in (24cm).
For border 1, cut four pieces 3½in (9cm) square.
FROM FABRIC C CUT THE FOLLOWING:
For border 4, cut four pieces 33½in (85cm) and four pieces 24½in (62cm).
For border 3, cut four pieces 3½in (9cm) square.
FROM FABRIC D CUT THE FOLLOWING:
For the central panel, cut five pieces 15½in (39.5cm), twelve pieces 9½in (24cm), six pieces 6½in (16.5cm) and sixteen pieces 3½in (9cm) square.
For border 4, cut four pieces 3½in (9cm) square.
FROM FABRIC E CUT THE FOLLOWING:
For the central panel, cut twelve pieces 3½in (9cm) square.
FROM FABRIC F CUT THE FOLLOWING:
For border 2, cut eight pieces 3½in (9cm) square.
FROM FABRIC G CUT THE FOLLOWING:
For the central panel and border 4, cut six pieces 3½in (9cm) square.
FROM FABRIC H CUT THE FOLLOWING:
For the central panel, cut eight pieces 3½in (9cm) square.

TO ASSEMBLE THE CENTRAL PANEL

4   Assemble the rows for the central panel, referring to the assembly diagram (Fig 1).
You will see that there are 17 rows in the central panel:
rows 1 and 17 are the same;
rows 2, 4, 8, 10, 14 and 16 are the same;
rows 3, 9 and 15 are the same;
rows 5, 7, 11 and 13 are the same;
rows 6 and 12 are the same.
Lay out the strips in order on the floor so that you are sure that you are joining the right ones. Stitch each row in turn taking a $1/4$in (5mm) seam allowance. Press all the seams towards the darker side.

5   Lay the completed rows out on the floor again, in the correct order, to check that you have assembled them correctly. Beginning from the top, join the rows with a $1/4$in (5mm) seam allowance. Press all the seams towards the darker side.

TO ASSEMBLE THE BORDERS

6   To make border 1, using a $1/4$in (5mm) seam allowance throughout, join the $51^{1}/2$in (131cm) strips of fabric A to the sides of the central panel. Join one square of fabric B to each end of the two $33^{1}/2$in (85cm) strips of fabric A, then join these two strips to the top and bottom of the central panel (see Fig 2).

7   To make border 2, assemble the side strips following Fig 3 and join them to the sides of the patchwork. Assemble the top and bottom strips as shown, and join them to the top and bottom of the patchwork.

8   To make border 3, join the $63^{1}/2$in (157cm) strips of fabric A to the sides of the patchwork. Join one square of fabric C to the ends of the $45^{1}/2$in (116cm) strips of fabric A, then add these strips to the top and bottom of the patchwork (see Fig 4).

9   To make border 4, assemble the side strips following Fig 5 and join them to the sides of the patchwork. Assemble the top and bottom strips as shown, and join them to the top and bottom of the patchwork. The piecing of your quilt top is now complete.

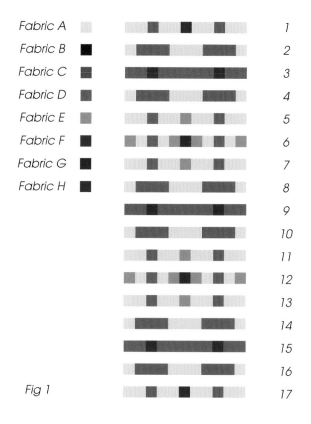

Fabric A — 1
Fabric B — 2
Fabric C — 3
Fabric D — 4
Fabric E — 5
Fabric F — 6
Fabric G — 7
Fabric H — 8
— 9
— 10
— 11
— 12
— 13
— 14
— 15
— 16
Fig 1 — 17

TO FINISH THE QUILT

10   Lay the backing right side up on a flat surface, then lay the quilt top, right side down, on top of the backing. Carefully position the wadding on the back of the quilt top. Pin and tack around the edges of all three layers, leaving an opening of about 18in (46cm) for turning. Stitch a $1/4$in (5mm) seam around the tacked edges. Turn the quilt top right side out, and slipstitch the opening closed.

11   Smooth out the quilt so that all the layers are flat and even, then tack a line $1/4$in (5mm) in from the edge. Stitch around this line with machine straight stitch, or with hand running stitch in quilting thread.

12   Lay the quilt flat again, and tack with a grid of horizontal and vertical lines as usual for quilting (see page 14). Sew the buttons on in the positions marked in Fig 6, stitching right through to the back of the quilt. If you prefer, quilt the layers with knots: stitch lengths of strong thread through all the layers, tie them in reef knots on the surface, and cut the ends into tufts.

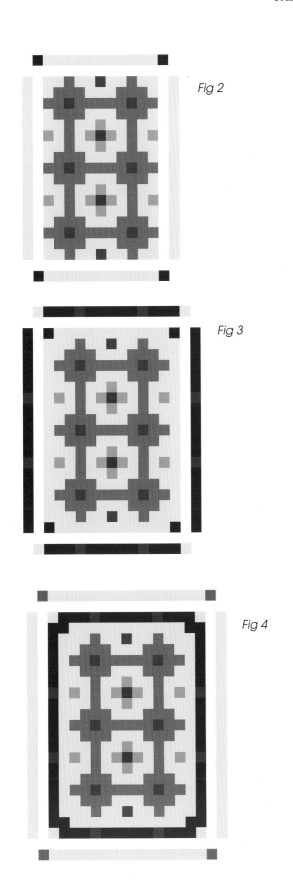

Fig 2

Fig 3

Fig 4

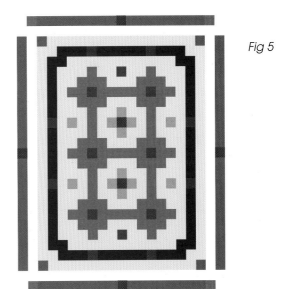

Fig 5

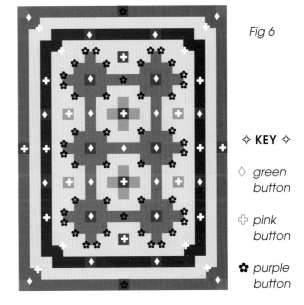

Fig 6

✧ **KEY** ✧

◇ green
button

✚ pink
button

❀ purple
button

PRACTICAL TIPS

✧ A rotary cutter is very useful for cutting the
original strips accurately. If you position the
fabrics on top of each other carefully, you can
cut all the first 3¹/₂in (9cm) strips together.

✧ Because the wadding is already held in place by
the outside stitching and won't move very much,
if you prefer you can just hold the layers of the
quilt together with safety pins instead of tacking
while you stitch the buttons on.

SASHIKO

Sashiko (pronounced 'sash-ko') quilting is a Japanese technique which has become popular with western quilters over the past few years. Sashiko, a sort of cross between quilting and embroidery, involves creating geometric patterns – often several different patterns on each project – using large running stitches. The technique was traditionally used on kimonos, among other things, in a traditional colour scheme of white on blue.

It is very easy to transfer the sashiko technique for use in Celtic designs, as I've done for the projects in this section. Even complex knot designs can be stitched very easily in sashiko quilting. The blue card on page 92 combines a simple knot outline with a traditional sashiko filling design of equilateral triangles. The long flowing lines of spiral designs can be emphasised to great effect with the strong sashiko stitches. The needlecase on page 94 uses a vivid red spiral design on a printed background fabric. The complicated lines of animal and bird designs are easy to work in sashiko; any of the bird designs in this book would look equally good in the technique.

Geometric key patterns seem to have been made for this kind of stitching. The teacosy on page 97 uses a simple key pattern and motif in the traditional colour scheme of white on blue, while the tablecloth on page 99 makes use of a more complex key design that is then thrown into relief by outline stitching and seeding. The

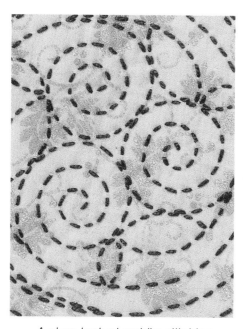

A close look at sashiko stitching

aquamarine card on page 92 uses an unusual seven-section circular key pattern.

SASHIKO STITCHING

Unlike traditional quilting, where the stitches are really only there to create patterns by dimpling the wadding, the stitches in sashiko are an important part of the finished effect. They are meant to show, and are usually worked in a colour that contrasts with the backing fabric.

The basic sashiko stitch is a sizeable running stitch, worked so that the stitch is twice as long on the surface as it is underneath (see Fig A). Special white sashiko thread can be bought that looks good on dark backgrounds, or you can use coton à broder or thin coton perlé for a similar effect. Crochet cotton also works well and is economical. The bedcover on page 103 is worked in ordinary quilting thread. For special effects you can try working the stitch in metallic thread, or a multicoloured thread – both of these look particularly effective on dark backgrounds.

PADDING

Sashiko quilting is usually worked through one or more layers of fabric, but is not always padded with extra wadding. When just two layers are used there is a slightly quilted effect where the two layers are pulled together. Japanese stitchers sometimes quilted sashiko items with a thin layer of silk wadding; this is expensive, but gives a lovely effect, especially if the top fabric is also silk. Try this for an exclusive evening jacket or on the embroidered bodice of a wedding dress. A cheaper way of achieving a similar effect is with dolmette, which is a fairly flat but quite heavy padding fabric. You could also use a thin layer of polyester wadding. Some retailers are now selling denser polyester waddings which are good for making quilted clothes without adding too much bulk. For warmth and not too much padding in your sashiko garment or bed quilt, try a layer of Viyella fabric or a thin curtain lining.

STITCHING LINES

Accurate stitching lines are very important in sashiko projects because the lines are usually geometric patterns, and because the stitching is so visible. It quickly becomes obvious if a corner isn't sharp or a curve isn't smooth. Make sure that your design is always marked accurately. Use a fading pen, a water-soluble pen, or a sharp crayon slightly lighter than your background fabric so that the marks will disappear as you stitch. Try to take several stitches with each passage of the needle, so that you get into a rhythm.

If you are stitching a design with numerous sharp angles, either stitch them all so that there is always a small gap at each point (see Fig B), or so that two stitches meet at each point (see Fig C). If you mix the two techniques in one design the angles will look uneven. If your design has several stitching lines crossing, try and work the stitches so that there is a small gap where the lines cross (see Fig D); if the actual stitches cross, the stitching will look too dense and rather untidy at that point (see Fig E). If you want to keep the back of your work free from knots, secure the thread invisibly before you start stitching.

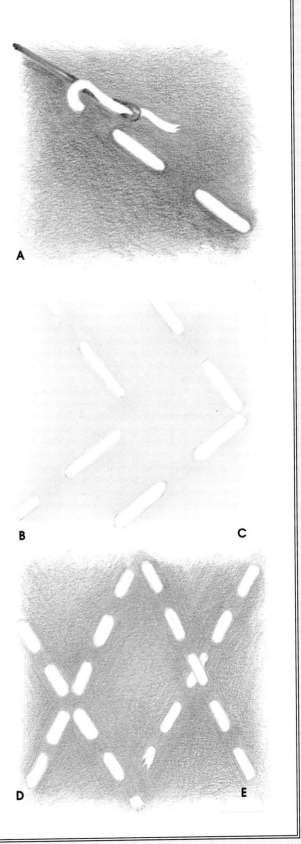

A

B

C

D

E

SASHIKO GREETINGS CARDS

Three different types of Celtic design are featured in these unusual all-occasion greetings cards. The first design is a simple knot, worked with a sashiko pattern inside the knot itself; the second features a circular key pattern, and the third has a design built up from three animal heads. Animals like these appear quite often in Celtic art, and seem to be half lion, half dog. They often have quaint spiral noses, contrasting with their slightly fierce bared teeth!

SIZE OF FINISHED DESIGNS: knot 3¹/₂ x 5in (9 x 12.5cm); circular key pattern 5¹/₂in (14cm) diameter; animal design 5¹/₂in (14cm) diameter

MATERIALS

FOR THE KNOT CARD:

- ❖ *Purple-blue silk, 6 x 8in (15 x 20cm)*
- ❖ *Thin wadding or dolmette the same size*
- ❖ *Cream card mount with a rectangular aperture 3³/₄ x 5³/₄in (9.5 x 14.5cm)*
- ❖ *Coton à broder, one skein each in pale blue and pink*
- ❖ *Medium sewing needle*

FOR THE KEY-PATTERN CARD:

- ❖ *Pale aquamarine silk, 9in (23cm) square*
- ❖ *Thin wadding or dolmette the same size*

- *Large white card mount with a circular aperture 6in (15cm) in diameter*
- *Coton à broder, one skein mid purple*
- *Medium/large sewing needle*

FOR THE ANIMAL CARD:
- *Aquamarine silk, 9in (23cm) square*
- *Thin wadding or dolmette the same size*
- *Large white card mount with a circular aperture 6in (15cm) in diameter*
- *Coton à broder, one skein dark purple*
- *Medium/large sewing needle*

FOR ALL DESIGNS:
- *Paper for tracing*
- *Black felt-tip pen*
- *Crayons in purple, pale blue and pink*
- *Tacking needle and thread*
- *Craft glue*

PRODUCING THE DESIGNS

1 Enlarge the designs on this page to the correct size (see page 12), and go over the lines with thick black felt pen to make them darker. Press the silk pieces and lay them over the appropriate designs, and trace the lines with sharp crayon, using blue and pink for the knot design and purple for each of the other two designs.

2 Tack the pieces of dolmette or wadding behind each design. For the knot card, work sashiko stitching over all the lines of the leaf shape in pink coton à broder, then go round the outlines only of the knot shape (not the background pattern) whipping the stitches with another strand of pink (see page 13). This strengthens the outline. Stitch the twisted shape in pale blue, then whip the outlines in the same way (see page 13).

3 For the key pattern, work sashiko stitching around all the lines using the mid purple coton à broder thread.

4 On the animal design, stitch round all the lines in dark purple coton à broder.

5 Lay the stitched designs face down on a soft surface, such as a thick towel, and press from the back. Trim each design to fit its card blank, then assemble as for the cards on page 17.

5¹/₂in (14cm)

If you are using a photocopier enlarge by 200%

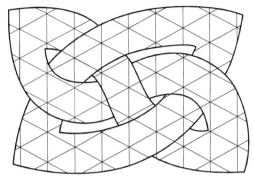

Knot design

Key design

Animal design

RED AND GOLD NEEDLECASE

The strong lines of sashiko seem to require dramatic designs; this red spiral design make a real splash on the front of a needlecase. Choose a slightly patterned fabric to add a bit of texture to the background, then pick a toning colour of felt for the 'leaves' inside which hold the needles.

SIZE OF FINISHED NEEDLECASE: 6in (15cm) square

MATERIALS

❖ *White and gold patterned cotton fabric, 1/4yd (25cm) by at least 25in (65cm) wide*
❖ *White felt, one piece 5 x 10in (12.5 x 25cm), one piece 4 x 8in (10 x 20cm)*
❖ *Dolmette or fusible wadding, 6 x 12in (15 x 30cm)*
❖ *Gold machine stitching thread, eg Madeira No. 40 gold 4*
❖ *Skein of red coton perlé No. 5*

❖ *Large sharp needle*
❖ *White or cream sewing thread*
❖ *Water-soluble pen*
❖ *Black felt-tip pen*

PRODUCING THE DESIGN

1 Wash and press the cotton fabric, then cut two rectangles 6½ x 12½in (16 x 31cm). Fold one piece in half, right sides out. Using a water-soluble pen, draw in the seam allowances of ¼in (5mm) on each of the raw edges, which will leave a 6in (15cm) square. Mark the diagonals of the square in water-soluble pen.

2 Trace the pattern below, then go over the lines with the black pen to make them darker. Position the marked square over the pattern so that the design is centred and then trace the lines in water-soluble pen.

❖ VARIATIONS ❖
This design works well as a repeat pattern. Try edging it with a square border, then repeating it as a border or alternating it with plain squares in a chequer pattern. It would also look effective greatly enlarged and worked in the four quarters of a double bed quilt.

3 Tack the piece of dolmette onto the back of the fabric, or fuse on the fusible wadding with a warm iron.

4 Using the red coton perlé in a large needle, stitch the lines in sashiko quilting (see page 91), keeping the curves smooth and the points sharp. When the stitching is complete, spray the design with cold water to remove the water-soluble pen marks. Allow to dry completely.

5 Lay the design face down on a soft surface and press. Put the two rectangles of cotton fabric right sides together and stitch a $^1/_4$in (5mm) seam around the two long edges and the front edge. Clip the corners and turn the design right side out. Press the very edges only. Fold under the seam allowance on the remaining edge and

tack, then using gold thread, topstitch all round the rectangle, $^1/_8$in (2mm) in from the edges, to close the gap and add a little bit of decoration.

6 Cut the felt pieces with pinking shears to give decorative edges. Fold the two pieces in half down the centre and press to set the folds. Open the needlecase and lay it on a flat surface with the lining upwards. Put the large piece of felt on top of the lining so that the folds align and there is an even border top and bottom, then put the smaller piece of felt on top of the larger piece in the same way. Tack the three layers in position down the fold line. Fold the needlecase shut, and topstitch $^1/_8$in (2mm) in from the fold line in gold to seal in the felt pieces. Remove the tacking thread from the work.

INDIGO TEACOSY

The traditional sashiko colour scheme of white-on-blue is used for this teacosy. This was a favourite Japanese colourway for daytime kimonos, which were made from fabric dyed with indigo. The key design appears as a border and as a square motif, where the individual motif is turned 'on point' to give it a different dynamic.

SIZE OF FINISHED TEACOSY: 17 x 12$\frac{1}{2}$in (43 x 32cm)

MATERIALS
- ❖ *Firm blue jacquard cotton furnishing fabric, $\frac{1}{2}$yd (50cm) by at least 40in (100cm) wide*
- ❖ *Pale blue lining fabric, the same size*
- ❖ *2oz wadding, the same size*
- ❖ *Dolmette, 16 x 12in (41 x 31cm)*
- ❖ *One skein of white coton perlé No. 5*
- ❖ *Medium/large sewing needle*
- ❖ *Dark blue sewing thread*
- ❖ *Tacking needle and thread*
- ❖ *Pencils and paper for drawing the design*
- ❖ *Dressmakers' carbon paper in pale blue*

PRODUCING THE DESIGN

1 Enlarge the design and curved shape on page 98 to the correct size (see page 12).

2 Use the curved shape to cut two pieces from the blue jacquard, two pieces of wadding, and two pieces from the pale blue lining fabric.

3 Pin the carbon paper, carbon side down, onto the right side of one of the jacquard pieces. Pin the design on top so that the straight edge of the pattern is 2in (5cm) from the bottom of the blue fabric and parallel with it, and so that there is an even border of fabric at each end of the design. Centre the single motif 'on point' just above the border. Go over the lines of the designs with pencil to transfer them. Unpin the papers.

4 Lay the dolmette on a flat surface and place the marked jacquard piece, right side up, on top. Tack the two layers together near the edges of the designs. Using the white coton perlé, work sashiko stitching (see page 90) round all the lines

of the border and the single motif. Remove the tacking threads and trim the dolmette to fit the teacosy shape. Lay the design face down on a soft surface and press gently from the back.

5 Trim 1in (2.5cm) off the straight edges of the wadding shapes. Lay one piece of wadding on a flat surface and cover it with one piece of lining, right side up. Follow this with the other piece of lining, wrong side up, and the second piece of wadding. Pin, tack and stitch the four layers together around the curved edge, taking a $\frac{1}{2}$in (1.2cm) seam allowance. Trim the seam allowances close to the stitching line.

6 Put the two pieces of jacquard right sides together, then pin, tack and stitch a $\frac{1}{2}$in (1.2cm) seam around the curved edge. Trim and clip the seam allowances, turn right side out and press the edges of the teacosy shape to set the seam. Slip this shape over the inner shape so that the wadding is between the jacquard and the lining and the raw edges match at the bottom.

7 Turn the edge of the jacquard fabric under $\frac{1}{4}$in (5mm) and press. Turn the raw edges of the lining and wadding inwards by about 1in (2.5cm), then fold the edges of the jacquard over the lining by $\frac{1}{2}$in (1.2cm). Pin and tack the folded edges in position, then stitch into place by hand or machine.

PRACTICAL TIP
- ✧ *If there are any marks from the carbon paper still visible when the stitching is finished, rub the stitched area gently with a small offcut of the jacquard fabric to remove them.*

✧ VARIATIONS ✧
The key border can be extended if you wish, for instance for a larger project such as a tablecloth or sideboard runner. Simply ignore the lines at one end of the panel and continue adding key patterns to the required length. Then stitch the end lines to finish off the design.

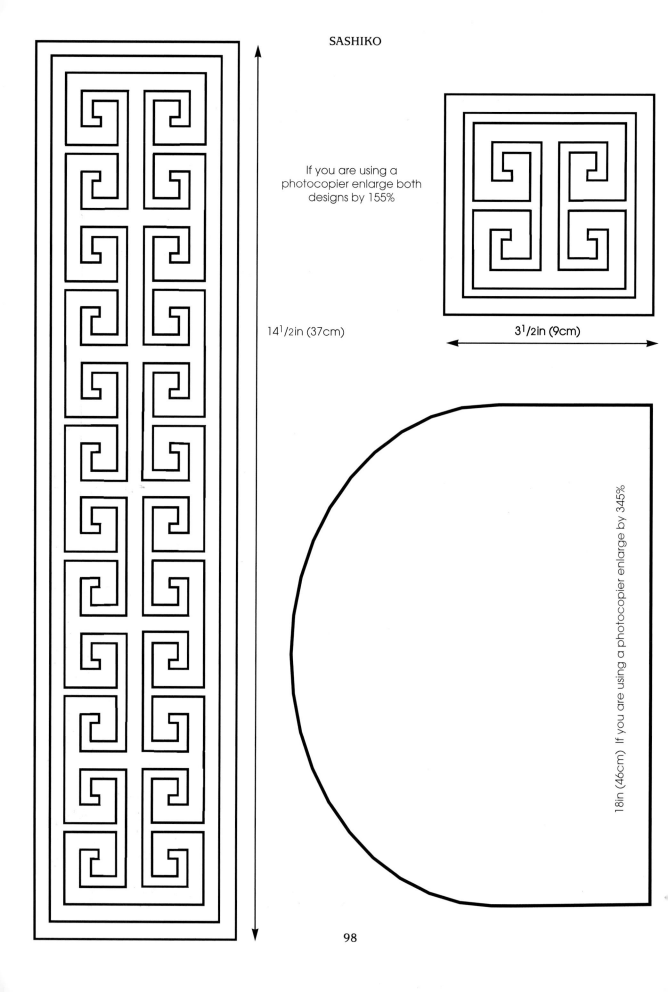

If you are using a
photocopier enlarge both
designs by 155%

14^1/2in (37cm)

3^1/2in (9cm)

18in (46cm) If you are using a photocopier enlarge by 345%

GEOMETRIC TABLECLOTH

The striking design in the centre of this tablecloth is a square key pattern. The main lines are stitched in mid green coton à broder, then the outlines are echoed with dark green stitching. The internal spaces created by the design are filled with yellow seeding stitches. The stitchery is padded slightly by using two layers of fabric – a small, square white damask cloth is laid over a larger pale yellow cloth, and the design stitches the two together, producing a slightly quilted effect.

Size of finished design: 14¹/₂in (37cm)

MATERIALS

* *One small white damask tablecloth, 35in (90cm) square*
* *One pale yellow cotton or cotton/polyester tablecloth, 50in (128cm) square*
* *Coton à broder, one skein each in mid green, dark green and mid yellow*
* *Medium sewing needle*
* *Tacking needle and thread*
* *Water-soluble pen*
* *Pencils, paper and black felt-tip pen for drawing the design*

PRODUCING THE DESIGN

1 Enlarge the design on page 101 to the correct size, then go over the lines with black felt-tip pen to make them darker.

2 Press the white damask tablecloth, then fold it in half lengthways and then widthways and press the folds to mark them. Lay the design on a flat surface then unfold the damask and place it, right side up, over the design so that the corners of the pattern lie on the folds of the damask and the design forms a diamond shape in the centre of the tablecloth. Draw the lines of the design on the damask with the water-soluble pen.

3 Lay the yellow tablecloth on a flat surface, right side up, and position the damask tablecloth, marked side up, on top of it so that there is an even border all round. Tack the two layers together near the outside of the design, and work a few lines of tacking across the design in each direction to secure the cloths together.

4 Using the mid green coton à broder, work sashiko stitching (see page 90) along all the lines of the design. Begin with the central square and work outwards along the key pattern. Keep the stitches even, and make sure that the points of the corners and of the other angles are sharp (see page 91).

5 When all the lines of the design are stitched, work a line of dark green stitching about 1/8in (2mm) outside the outer border, and just inside all of the internal triangles and the central square (see photograph below).

6 Using the yellow coton à broder, work seeding stitches (see page 13) randomly inside the central square and inside each internal triangle.

7 When all the stitching is complete, spray the design with cold water to remove the water-soluble pen marks and allow to dry completely. If all the marks have not vanished when the fabric has dried, simply spray again. When the fabric is totally dry, lay the design face down on a soft surface and press it from the back with a steam iron.

PRACTICAL TIPS

✧ *If you want to keep the back of your work very neat, begin each new thread with a small knot and pull it through the backing fabric so that it is concealed between the two layers of the white and yellow tablecloths.*

✧ *Don't pull the thread too tightly on the seeding stitches, otherwise you will make the fabric pucker. Leave the thread quite loose as you move from one part of the design to another.*

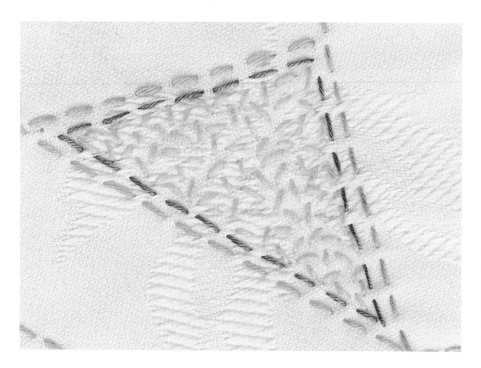

This detail shows the echo stitching in dark green and the yellow seeding worked in one of the internal triangles created by the design

14¹/2in (37cm) If you are using a photocopier enlarge by 225%

✧ VARIATIONS ✧
These key designs look their best worked in
sashiko. Try this one in pale threads on a dark
silk cushion, or work several blocks in a repeat
pattern across a full-size quilt.

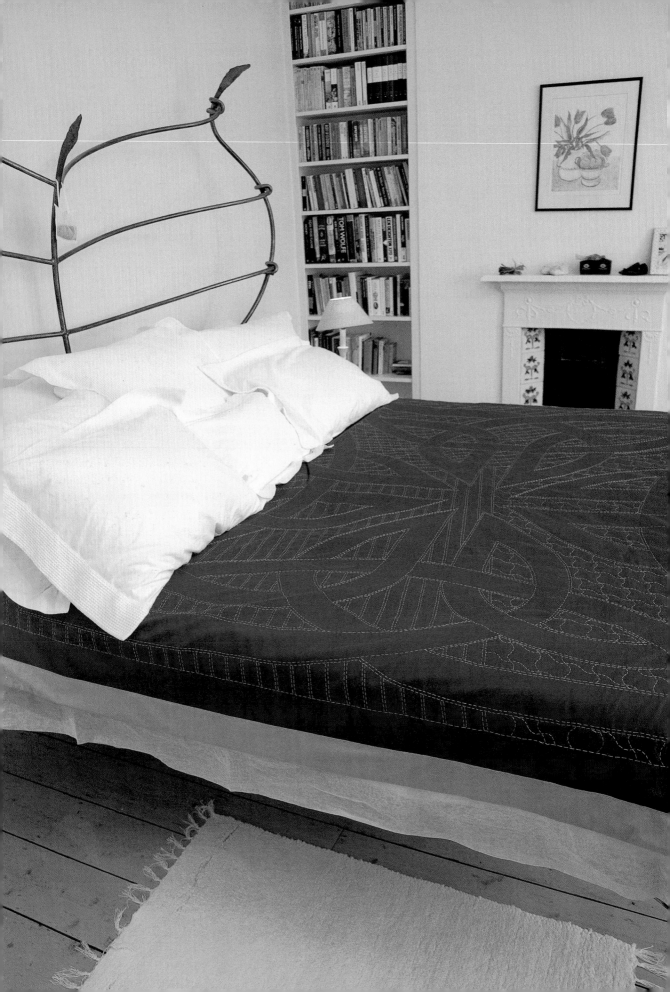

SASHIKO BED QUILT

A large square knot decorates this double bed quilt, thrown into relief by the sashiko patterning behind it. The patterns follow the tradition of sashiko design in which the stitching area is divided asymmetrically by straight lines, each division then being filled with a different geometric pattern. Two layers of sheeting are used to give a slightly padded effect to the stitching, but you could add a layer of thin wadding for extra warmth if you wish.

SIZE OF FINISHED QUILT: 86in (220cm) square

MATERIALS

- ❖ *Maroon fabric, 82in (208cm) square*
- ❖ *Mauve fabric, 92in (234cm) square*
- ❖ *Two reels of white quilting thread*
- ❖ *Mauve sewing thread*
- ❖ *Medium sewing or quilting needle*
- ❖ *Quilting frame (optional)*
- ❖ *Marking pencil for dark fabrics*
- ❖ *Pencil, paper and black felt-tip pen for drawing the design*

PRODUCING THE DESIGN

1 Wash and press the fabric squares.

2 Enlarge the design on page 104 to the correct size, then go over the lines with black felt-tip pen to make them darker.

3 Lay the tracing on a large flat surface and lay the maroon fabric on top – you should be able to see the design lines faintly through the fabric. If not, tape the design across a large window on a sunny day, to act as a natural lightbox. Position the fabric so that there is an even border all around the design. Pin the fabric and tracing together, then go over all the design lines with the marking pencil. Remove the pins.

4 The straight lines divide the design into three sections. Use the sashiko patterns on pages 105–107 to trace a different pattern behind the knot in each section.

5 Lay the mauve fabric on a flat surface, right side down, and lay the maroon square, marked side up, on top so that there is an even border of mauve all around the edges. Pin in position. Tack the two layers together at regular intervals – roughly 2–3 inches (5–8cm) apart – using a grid of horizontal and vertical tacking lines (see page 14). Remove the pins.

6 Using the white quilting thread (and a quilting frame if you wish, see page 12), work sashiko stitching (see page 90) around all the main lines of the knot. Begin in the centre of the design and work outwards. Then stitch echo lines 1/4in (5mm) outside the knot edges. When the knot is complete, stitch the outer edge of the sashiko background and the lines dividing the different patterns. Finally, stitch along all the lines of the sashiko background patterns. Remove the tacking threads.

7 Lay the design face down on a flat surface and press from the back. Fold over a hem of about 1/2in (1cm) onto the front of the mauve fabric, then fold over a second hem of about 2 1/2in (6.5cm) to cover the raw edges of the maroon fabric. Tack, then stitch in place by hand or machine, removing the tacking threads when you have finished.

PRACTICAL TIPS

✧ *Polyester/cotton sheeting comes in very wide widths and is ideal for this project. Alternatively, you can buy ready-made flat sheets in the appropriate colours.*

✧ *For neatness on the reverse side of the final quilt, begin each thread with a knot and pull it through the background fabric so that it is hidden between the layers of fabric.*

✧ VARIATIONS ✧

This quilt can be worked in any colour scheme. For a completely different effect try dark stitching on a pale background.
If you wish, you can divide the background into more sections and add more sashiko designs.

70in (180cm)

NOTES TO HELP YOU DRAW THE COMPLETE DESIGN:
Draw the knot and its border onto your fabric first, then add the straight lines A-B and C-D (on the background only, as shown) to divide the design into three sections. Draw pattern 1 onto the background of the section marked (behind the knot), with the lines all parallel with line C-D. Draw pattern 2 onto the section marked in the same way, with the design parallel to line A-B. Fill the remaining section with pattern 3.

PATTERN 1

PATTERN 2

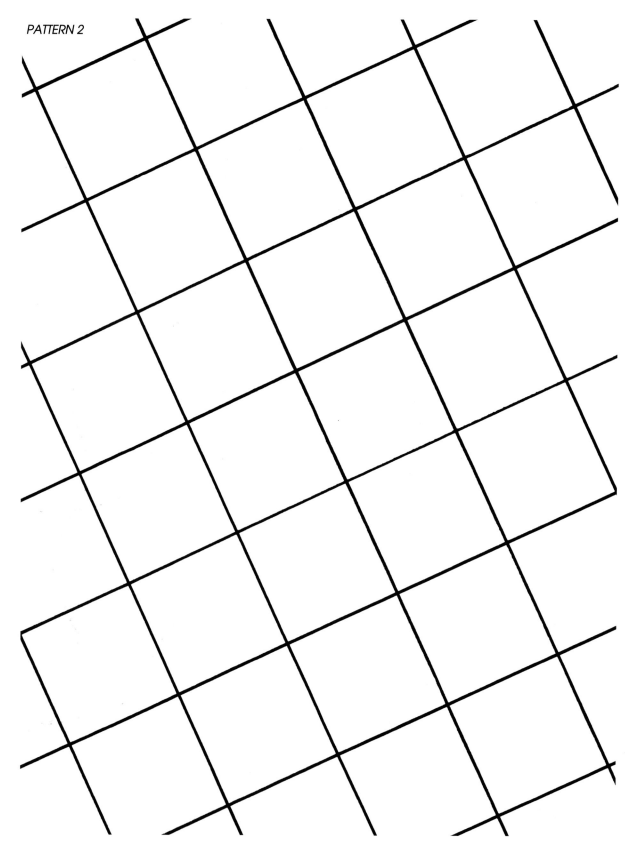

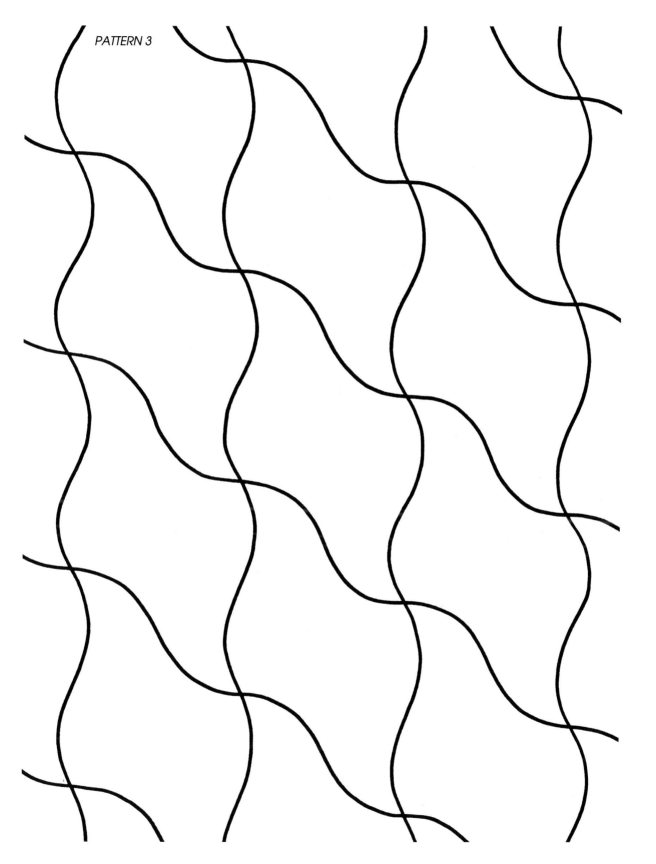

PATTERN 3

PATTERN LIBRARY

KNOTS

KNOTS

KNOTS

KNOTS

KNOTWORK BORDERS

KNOTWORK BORDERS

KNOTWORK BORDERS

KNOTWORK BORDERS

SPIRAL DESIGNS

SPIRAL DESIGNS

FRET AND KEY PATTERNS

FRET AND KEY PATTERNS

ALPHABETS

ALPHABETS

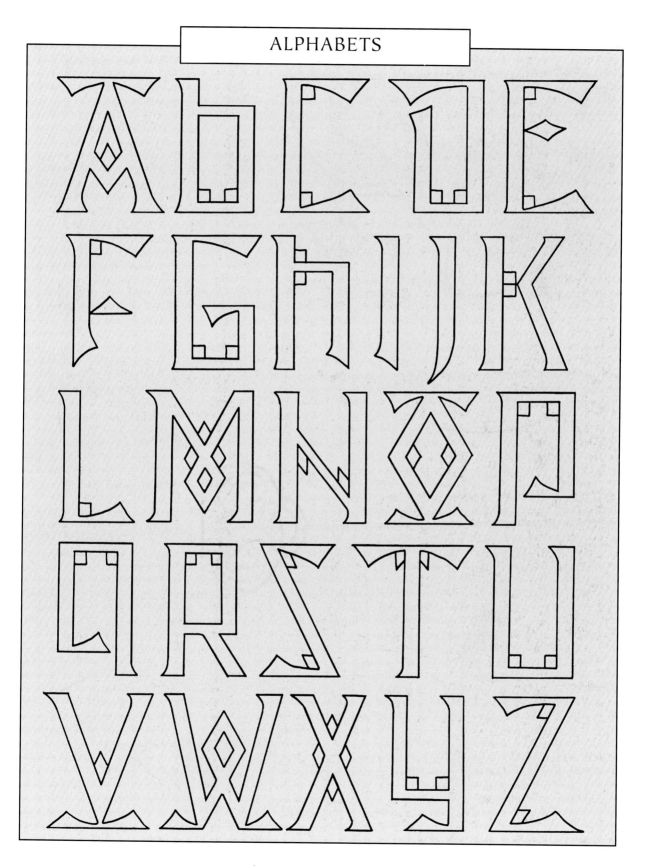

CARPET PAGE DESIGNS

CARPET PAGE DESIGNS

ANIMALS, BIRDS AND FISH

ANIMALS, BIRDS AND FISH

PLANT DESIGNS

ACKNOWLEDGEMENTS

Many thanks to my mother, Angela Besley, for
expertly stitching the workbox, the footstool and
the child's bed quilt; to Anna Carey for her clear
and skilful illustrations; and to Carole Coren for
producing so many of the excellent charts from
my scribbles!

BIBLIOGRAPHY

If you would like to design your own Celtic
quilting patterns, or to know more about Celtic art,
the following books are recommended:

Celtic Design: Knotwork
Celtic Design: Animal Patterns
Celtic Design: Illuminated Letters
Celtic Design: a Beginner's Manual
All by Aidan Meehan, published by Thames &
Hudson 1992
Celtic Knotwork Designs by Sheila Sturrock,
published by Guild of Master Craftsman
Publications Ltd 1997
Celtic Stencil Designs by Co Spinhoven, published
by Dover 1990
Decorative Celtic Alphabets by Mallory Pearce,
published by Dover 1992
Celtic Art: the Methods of Construction by George
Bain, published by Constable 1992

Celtic Knotwork by Iain Bain, published by
Constable 1992
Celtic Key Patterns by Iain Bain, published by
Constable 1993
*Art in Wales 2000 BC-AD 1850, an illustrated
history* edited by Eric Rowan, published by Welsh
Arts Council/University of Wales Press 1978
Celtic and Anglo-Saxon Painting by Carl
Nordenfalk, published by Chatto & Windus 1977
Celtic Cross Stitch by Gail Lawther, published by
David & Charles 1996
*The Celtic Vision: selections from the Carmina
Gadelica* edited by Esther de Waal, published by
Darton, Longman and Todd 1988
The Lindisfarne Gospels by Janet Backhouse,
published by Phaidon 1994
Decorative Patterns of the Ancient World by
Flinders Petrie, published by Studio Editions 1990

INDEX

Page numbers in *italic* refer to illustrations

Adapting Celtic designs, 6
Animal, bird and fish designs,
    10–11, 16–17, *17, 28,* 29–31,
    40–3, *41,* 48–53, *49, 50,* 90,
    92–3, 124–25
Appliqué, 6–7, 8, 9, 32–53

Backstitch, 13, 54
Bias binding, 8, 32, 48–51
Bibliography, 127
Birds Sofa Throw, 29–31
Book of Durrow, 6
Book of Kells, 6
Border designs, 7, 9, 24–7, 65–7,
    97–8, 112–19, 126
Bridal Handbag, 65–7, *65*
Bright Cushion, 74–5, *74*

Carpet page patterns, 9–10, 37–9,
    72, 74–5, 86–9, *87,* 122–23
Celtic art and design, 6, 7, 8–11, 32,
    54, 72, 90, 92, 127
Celtic Cross Stitch, 6
Centring designs, 12
Chain stitch, 13, 54
Child's Bed Quilt, *72,* 86–9, *87*
Corded quilting, 6–7, 8, 11, 54–71
Covering a box with fabric, 68–71

Dragon picture, 40–3, *41*

Enlarging designs, 12

Fabrics for patchwork and quilting,
    9, 11–12, 14, 19, 32, 40, 45,
    54, 82
Fret and key designs, 6, 9–10, 14,
    16–17, *17,* 76–81, 90, 92–3, *96,*
    97–101, *99, 100,* 118–19

General techniques, 12–13
Geometric Tablecloth, 99–102, *99,*
    100; Table-mats, 76–8, *77*
Greetings cards, wholecloth, 16–17,
    18; Sashiko, 92–3, *92*

Hand-quilting, 15, 16–17, 19–27,
    29–31, 44–7, 54, 56–64, 68–71,
    90–107
Herb Pillow, *54,* 62–4, *62*

Indigo Teacosy, *96,* 97–8
Initial Pictures, 58–61, *58*

Key-pattern Footstool, 79–81, *79*
Knot designs, 6–10, 14, 16–17,
    19–21, 24–7, 32–6, 44–7, *54,*
    56–72, 82–5, 90, 92–3, 102–15;
    Pram Quilt, *14,* 24–7, *25;* Trinket
    Box, 68–71, *69*

Ladder stitch, 13
Lettering, 11, 58–61, *58,* 72, 120–1,
    120–1
Lindisfarne Gospels, 6

Machine appliqué, 6, 10, 32–43,
    48–53; patchwork, 72–81,
    86–89; quilting, 11, 15, 54, 65–7
Making up, 12
Marking designs, 12
Methods of quilting, 6–7
Mitring corners, 78

Patchwork, 6–8, 10–11, 72–89, *72;*
    Work-bag, 82–5, *82*
Pattern library, 6, 55, 108–26
Piecing over papers, 6, 72–3, 82–5
Pressing quilting and piecing, 55, 73

Quilting equipment, 11–12; frame,
    12; methods, 6–7; with beads
    and buttons, 74–5, 86–9

Red and Gold Needlecase, *90,* 94–6,
    95, 96
Rotary cutter, 11, 51, 89
Running stitch, 6, 13, 15, 16, 73, 90

Sashiko, 7–12, 14, 90–107; Bed
    Quilt, *102,* 103–7; Greetings
    Cards, 92–3, *92*
Seeding, 13, 64, 99–101
Shadow appliqué/quilting, 6, 8, 33,
    44–7, 55, 58–61; Cot Quilt,
    44–7, *44*
Sparkling Evening Bag, 37–9, *37, 38*
Spiral designs, 9, 14, 22–3, 65–7, 90,
    94–5, 116–17; Dolls' Quilt, 22–3, *22*
Stained glass appliqué, 6, 8, 11,
    32–3, 48–53; Wall Hanging,
    48–53, *49, 50*
Stitch library, 6, 13
Stitch 'n' Tear, 33, 40
Strip–piecing, 6, 72–3, 76–8
Sutton Hoo jewellery, 6

Tacking quilt layers together, 14–15
Threads for quilting, 12, 15, 32–3,
    64, 90
Trapunto (stuffed) quilting, 6, 8, 10,
    54–71, *54*
Triangular Pincushion, 56–7, *56*

Wadding, 6, 15, 91
Wedding Ring Cushion, 34–6, *34*
Whipped running stitch, 13, 54, 93
Wholecloth quilting, 6, 14–31; Silk
    Cushion, *18,* 19–21